P9-CJR-163

A Wounded Innocence

Sketches for a Theology of Art

Alejandro R. García-Rivera

A Michael Glazier Book

THE LITURGICAL PRESS
Collegeville, Minnesota

www.litpress.org

A Michael Glazier Book Published by The Liturgical Press

Cover design by David Manahan, O.S.B. *The Incredulity of St. Thomas* (1601–02) by Michelangelo Merisi da Caravaggio, 1573–1610, an oil painting now at the Neues Palais, Potsdam.

1 2 3 4 5 6 7 8

Library of Congress Cataloging-in-Publication Data

García-Rivera, Alex.
A wounded innocence : sketches for a theology of art / Alejandro R. García-Rivera.
p. cm.
Includes bibliographical references and index.
ISBN 0-8146-5112-7 (alk. paper)
1. Christianity and the arts. I. Title.

BR115.A8 G375 2003
261.5'7—dc21

2002031284

Contents

Illustrations

Foreword

Who else than Alejandro García-Rivera could bring together so many currents of culture and theology in a living, vibrant unity. To mention just some of them—the caves of Lascaux, Marcel Duchamp, Josiah Royce, Arthur Poulin's *Christmas Night at the Hermitage,* the stained-glass windows at St-Denis, St. Martin de Porres, and the Vietnam Memorial—makes one dizzy, at the edge of incomprehension. But, instead, one is taken on a road of discovery, to levels of living and lively perceptions that are more systematic and unified than traditional theologies, for they are addressed to the whole person.

For García-Rivera, theology is not of the essence of life if it is only a matter of intellectual construction. There are other sensibilities and lived experiences that belong to our humanness, so that passion and thought belong together. But it is also clear to him that such experiences take us to the natural alliance of beauty and justice. His Latin/Hispanic background provides a noble fragility, what he calls a wounded innocence, a posture in which one's hopes and failures, even rebellion, are known in a togetherness that is open to a grace that heals and enables. It is what art brings to the venture of theology. For example, all the facets of faith and community, that is, the full scope of what justification is about, are more aptly discovered and disclosed in the Vietnam Memorial than in treatises on justification.

The book is at once informative, full of surprises, convincing even when one wants to disagree, and a delight to read.

John Dillenberger
Professor Emeritus
Graduate Theological Union

Acknowledgments

I have many to thank. This book is the product of a long conversation that started a few years ago. My first thanks go to my students who have shared with me their life-giving enthusiasm and aptitude for wonder. I specially need to thank Mary Sue Ashbourne, Kate Bellm, Michelle Gonzalez, Michael Murphy, Nancy Pineda, and Greg Zuschlag who have looked carefully over the text (and even argued with me over some of the details). Few joys in life compare to the special relationship between student and teacher and writing this book has been an experience in joy. I also need to thank my colleagues here at the Graduate School of Religion and in other institutions. I am specially grateful to John Dillenberger for our conversations over coffee at the "Brewed Awakening" on Euclid Avenue. I also need to thank Jane Dillenberger, Doug Adams, and Michael Morris for their support of this boundary-crossing theologian into the field of the arts. I am truly indebted to my good friend and colleague, Don Gelpi, S.J., and the entire Courtney Murray group who in their annual meeting here at Berkeley discussed the book project with me. I am also thankful to John Markey, O.P., for his encouragement and helpful notes on the first chapter. I am also thankful to the members of the Academy of Catholic Hispanic Theologians (ACHTUS) who listened and gave helpful comments to a draft of the chapter on justification and sanctification this past summer. I am also deeply grateful to Fr. Arthur Poulin, O.S.B. Cam., and Fr. Robert Hale, O.S.B. Cam., for their wonderful conversations at Incarnation Monastery. Like the ancient monks who preserved a love of scholarship during a time of chaos, the Camaldolese are preserving a love of beauty and art. Indeed, this book was written by a community and I dare put my name on it only as one of many who have known a wounded innocence through their appreciation of the truly beautiful in art.

Introduction

Why an Interest in Theology and the Arts?

Why should theologians take the arts seriously? Those of us whose living context is Latin or Hispanic America have a ready answer.[1] An ancient issue was raised anew by Latin American theologians in the wake of Vatican II. Enrique Dussel first raised the issue as he started an ambitious but innovative project to document an authentic Latin American theology.[2] It was, at first, a practical issue: Where are the documents that describe an authentic Latin American theology? The commission soon came to the realization that the history of theology in Latin America began with missionary efforts from Europe and under the conquest of Imperial Spain. In other words, almost all the documents that usually chronicle a history had been made mostly by (and for) people in a position of power in the church or in Latin American society. These power brokers were rarely true Latin Americans. For this reason, as Dussel recounts, "Everywhere we were asked: A history of Latin American theology? Does such a theology exist? How do you make a history of the nonexistent?"[3]

What began as a practical issue soon became a question of theological method. As such, it was not a new issue. Irenaeus faced the same problem as the members of CEHILA in articulating the theology of the early Church in *Adverses Haereses*. The answer CEHILA gave to these questions was similar to Irenaeus.[4] "Yes," the members of CEHILA said, "an authentic Latin American theology exists although not in texts of theology. An authentic Latin American theology will be found in the symbols, rites, music, images, and stories of the living, Latin American Church."

For me, this answer came as a lightning stroke of insight. There exists a type of theology that could be called "living" as opposed to "textual." "Living theology" has its home in symbols, images, and songs. Theology lives in the music, imagery, and cultural symbols of those who must live out that which "textbook theology" attempts to understand. At this point, I do not want to be misunderstood. I am not disparaging textbook theology. I am simply saying it is insufficient in the study of a living faith. Let me make an analogy using an example from my freshman biology days. Dissecting the cadaver of a frog gives me some understanding of a frog but this understanding is insufficient to understand a living frog. Textbook theology dissects while living theology appreciates. Textbook theology provides understanding of the parts; living theology helps us appreciate the whole.

As I began to explore the living theology of Hispanic America by studying the symbols, imagery, and stories of the Latino community of faith (alongside a healthy dose of textbook theology!),[5] I also began to see that the CEHILA insight was the recovery of an ancient theological method and, thus, could be broadened. The first theologians of the Church looked at the symbols, imagery, and music of their living church in order to articulate their theology. What symbols, imagery, and music have in common is the aesthetic dimension.[6] If formality and rationality give substance to textbook theology, art and aesthetics animate a living theology. Convinced that aesthetics was the key to a living theology, a world of possibilities opened up to me in articulating a living theology. Not only symbols, images, and music but also poems, drama, and dance articulate a living theology. Here, I felt was a genuine contribution of the Latin American church that can be applied far beyond its boundaries. Aesthetics allows a look at the living theology not only of the church of Latin America, but also of the church of the United States, even, the church of Europe. As such, bringing the beautiful into theological reflection recovers an ancient way of doing theology and opens up a dimension of theology that has been little explored, indeed, cannot be explored by textbook theology.

Textbook Versus Living Aesthetics

As I began to explore the aesthetic dimension of a living theology, I found with dismay that aesthetics had also fallen on hard times in academic circles. There, too, one found the equivalent of a textbook theology. "Textbook aesthetics" tends to dissect the beautiful, much like textbook theology tends to dissect the faith of a living community. Textbook aesthetics isolated the beautiful in museums away from the living currents of society. More disturbing to me, it appeared that textbook aesthetics ignored or, worse, dismissed the theological dimension of beauty altogether. If textbook theology ignored the aesthetic dimension, then textbook aesthetics ignored the theological dimension. It began to dawn on me that perhaps there exists a "living aesthetics" similar to a "living theology."

As I began to explore this possibility, I made some initial observations. It appeared that textbook aesthetics, using my biology analogy, dissects the beautiful by separating the experience of beauty from the work of beauty. Textbook aesthetics tends toward dualisms between the work of art and the beholder, the artist and the community that appreciates his and her art, a work of art and a work of craft, the ugly and the beautiful, natural beauty and artistic beauty, and so on, and so forth. On the other hand, a living aesthetics sees a true continuity in the beautiful. The beautiful encompasses the ugly and the pretty, the grotesque and the ordinary, the artist and the artist's community, the work of art and the work of craft, the natural and that made by human hands. Indeed, a living aesthetics is less a disinterested beholding of some alienated object than that which moves the heart.

In the midst of these reflections on living theology and living aesthetics, I attended a workshop on theological education at the Wabash Center in Crawfordsville, Indiana. At a session, one of the young faculty in our group described his research project. He had asked the question that if the Greek culture was so visual, shouldn't the early Christian Church emerging out of the Greek culture also rely on the visual for its developing theology? His research thus far was showing the tremendous influence the visual played in the doctrinal and theological development of the early Church. His project astounded me. It seemed very similar to my own project with the Latin American church. It affirmed my belief that the CEHILA question was a fundamental question proper to all theology. More interesting, other people were now asking a similar question.

My time at Wabash raised some exciting questions for me. What might theology look like today if theologians, like my friend at Wabash, looked again at the contribution of the visual to the living theology of its day? The idea that a vast dimension of theology has been lost by discounting the visual both dismays and excites me. It dismays me for the fruitless debates and conundrums that an appreciation of the visual, of the arts, indeed, of the beautiful could have overcome. It excites me for I see that in having started to try to explore a particular question about the Latin American church, the Latin American question has turned out to be a genuine contribution to the whole Church in the discovery of the vital role of the visual dimension of a living theology.

Reasons for Writing This Book

The impetus for this book comes from trying to answer the following question: *what would happen if we took the visual seriously in theology?* I believe an answer to this question has the potential to significantly transform the shape of theology and theological education. The promise of this potential explains, in part, five major reasons for writing this book. First, if this potential is to be explored, the elements of a theology of art need to be discerned. Such theology must not be sidetracked by philosophical considerations of what art is or is not. It must concentrate on a theology of the human person for at the heart of the mystery of Beauty is the human capacity to experience it. What art is or is not will follow from this, not the other way around.

Second, I would like this book to also be a resource for the many artists who are my friends and those I have yet to meet who have more than a suspicion that their works contain profound insights into theology but do not have the language to articulate those insights. Third, I also hope this book gives encouragement to artists to produce works for the Church. The Church badly needs you. I hope that you will see in this work a heartfelt invitation to work together, theologians and artists, in mutual support towards the exploration of the depths of the human soul and the glory of the Lord. Fourth, I believe that taking the visual arts seriously may help advance the resolution of some knotty doctrinal questions such as the doctrine of justification. Various ecumenical dialogues have shown how pivotal linguistic misunderstandings have been in bitter doctrinal conflicts. There is a dimension of art, however, that articulates doctrinal insight in a way language cannot. Perhaps by recognizing and reflecting on works of art that address certain issues in doctrine, communities that doctrinal language has separated might find reconciliation in the aesthetics of the doctrine. Finally, I hope this book advances the work of Latin American and Hispanic theologians by broadening the scope and sweep of that fundamental insight from the Americas that theology is to be found as well in the "symbols, imagery, and music" of our living faith.

A New Theological Method

As described above, a theology of art calls for a new (actually, very old) way of doing theology. A theological method proper to a theology of art tends toward *synthesis*, putting things together, rather than *analysis*, taking things apart. A theology of art ought to understand the whole rather than the parts. Moreover, it ought to bring insight into the human condition rather than philosophical clarity as to the nature of art. Insight into the human condition means wrestling with the problem of suffering. Art, after all, does not take place in some isolated place away from the ordinary cares of the world but in the midst of the garden of good and evil. Given these considerations, a metaphor came to me that captured the spirit of such a theology of art. A theology of art concerns *a wounded innocence.*

This book attempts to sketch this intuited metaphor of a theology of art. As such, I am intentionally attempting a new (again, actually an ancient) method. Rather than give analytical, precise definitions, I am going to invite you to visit and revisit with me the metaphor of a "wounded innocence" in a series of reflections on selected works of art. I do not strive to "pin down" what a wounded innocence is but, rather, spiral into what it might be. This does not mean that the metaphor, a wounded innocence, is a construction. As I hope to demonstrate, the metaphor emerges out of the very tradition of the Church. A wounded innocence is not a construction, but names a mystery. Mystery invites the spiral approach rather than the linear, and a wounded innocence is, ultimately, a profound human mystery.

Mystery, however, does not imply a lack of knowledge nor does one attempt to understand a mystery without discipline and rigor. A synthetic approach to mystery does not mean an undisciplined approach. Indeed, artists may well be more disciplined and rigorous than mathematicians. The approach used in this book makes use of three disciplines: theology, philosophy, and history of art. I found that I could not do justice to a theology of art without combining these three disciplines in my sketches. The result, however, is not a perfectly balanced blend of the three disciplines. I am, by training and disposition, a theologian. The sketches do have a decidedly theological flavor. Nonetheless, I do not believe any of these disciplines can be ignored.

The study of the theological dimension in art requires knowledge of the philosophical issues raised, the historical context to be appreciated, and the theological tradition. It is the presence of all these three disciplines that prevents a theology of art from becoming disengaged from its subject. As such, the method used in this book takes some courage to apply. It is synthetic, provoking the analytically minded to frustration if they look for the parts instead of the whole. It is interdisciplinary leaving one open to *faux pas* in fields that are the result of self-study rather than formal training.[7] It is apologetic leaving the theologian open to the charge of compromising rigorous doctrine for the sake of reaching out to the "outsider."[8] Yet, I believe that in spite of all these dangers, the effort is well worth it.

A theology of art engages the world in a way other theologies can not. It promises to make a contribution to the understanding of believers and nonbelievers alike. It recovers for theology an ancient method that has been almost forgotten. More crucial, it promises insight into the human condition, the human engagement with beauty in the midst of great suffering. It promises an entry into the region that I call a wounded innocence.

1. By Hispanic America, I mean the living cultures that claim Hispanic descent and have a permanent basis within the political borders of the United States.

2. This project is known by the acronym CEHILA which, in English, stands for the Episcopal Commission for the History of the Church in Latin America and headed by Enrique Dussel. Although its intellectual origins date back to 1964, its creation came as a result of the 1972 meeting of Latin American Bishops (CELAM). The guidelines for CEHILA were laid down in their first meeting at Quito in 1973. Among these was a commitment to an ecumenical history in which both Protestant and Catholic contributions were sought. Another was a commitment to discern the authenticity and originality of a Latin American history of the Church. This meant a commitment to search for that history in nontraditional places as well as taking seriously a view of that history from the perspective of the socioeconomic poor. The account can be found in Pablo Richard, Carmelo Alvarez, and Comisión de Estudios de Historia de la Iglesia en Latinoamérica, *Raíces de la Teología Latinoamericana Nuevos Materiales para la Historia de la Teología*, edited by Pablo Richard (San José, Costa Rica: CEHILA Departamento Ecuménico de Investigaciones, 1985). Dussel's own description can be found in the prologue to Enrique Dussel, ed., *Introducción General a la Historia de la Iglesia en América Latina*, vol. 1 of *Historia General de la Iglesia en América Latina*, CEHILA (Salamanca: Ediciones Sígueme, 1983).

3. Pablo Richard, Enrique D. Dussel, Comisión de Estudios de Historia de la Iglesia en Latinoamérica, and Departamento Ecuménico de Investigaciones (Costa Rica), *Materiales para una Historia de la Teología en América Latina*, edited by Pablo Richard (San José, Costa Rica: Comisión de Estudios de Historia de la Iglesia en América Latina Departamento Ecuménico de Investigaciones, 1981) 7.

4. Irenaeus found his "documents" in the early liturgy of the Church, that is, in the creeds, rites, and hymns of the living Church.

5. This was the subject of my dissertation and it became my first book, *St. Martín de Porres the "Little Stories" and the Semiotics of Culture*, Faith and Cultures Series (Maryknoll, N.Y.: Orbis Books, 1995). In this book, I try to decipher a living theology of what it means to be human by studying the poetry and symbolism behind the "little stories" told about St. Martin de Porres at his beatification trial.

6. Hans Urs von Balthasar affirmed this conviction for me. In his seven volume theological aesthetics, he traces the use of aesthetics from the beginning of the Church to the present. Von Balthasar notes that in the patristic era, beauty was a guiding principle in theology, but after A.D. 1200, the beautiful dropped out of theology as part of its method.

7. I have formal training in theology and philosophy but I am mostly self-taught in art history.

8. Nonetheless, I must state directly that I am dealing here with questions of fundamental theology and not dogmatic theology. For this reason, I am not claiming the following to be official teachings of the Roman Catholic Church but fallible attempts to understand these teachings. I have tried to give the reader enough bibliography, however, to explore official Catholic teaching if so desired.

"The Wounded Hunter"

CHAPTER ONE

The Beginning of Art

The Cave of Lascaux

"I remember standing in front of the paintings of the horses facing the rhinos and being profoundly moved by the artistry. Tears were running down my cheeks. I was witnessing one of the world's great masterpieces."[1] Monsieur Jean Clottes, France's eminent expert on prehistoric art, so describes his first impressions of the Stone-Age paintings found deep within a cave at Lascaux, France. In light of Clottes' response, one wonders which is more impressive: that the first humans were capable of creating paintings of such striking beauty or that someone should be moved deeply by these ancient paintings thirty thousand years after their creation! Indeed, Clottes' response raises all sorts of philosophical questions not only about the nature of art but also about the nature of our humanity. Perhaps most enigmatic is the question Clottes raises about the relationship between religion and art. For, in his response, one finds the unmistakable signs of a deep, religious experience.

This ought not to surprise us. The entire cave at Lascaux gives strong evidence that it served a purely religious function. The cave at Lascaux appears to be not simply an ancient museum of art but a religious shrine of sorts. The paintings throughout the cave are organized as a temple or as an ordered whole of religious significance. As Joseph Campbell, the great scholar of myths and rituals puts it: "That the paintings of the Paleolithic caves cannot have been created to serve an exoteric function is obvious from the fact of their inaccessibility to general view. They are hidden, deeply hidden, to be approached only by way of dangerous, often very difficult passages."[2] In none of the Paleolithic caves found so far is this truer than at Lascaux. The minute we enter the cave of Lascaux, the heart stops and then races as it recognizes itself in a marvelous profusion of incredibly beautiful images. Bears, horses, rhinoceroses, ibexes, and even imaginary animals prance, gallop, and stand in awe-some majesty before our eyes. Perhaps the most incredible find as we begin our descent is this: Whoever created this incredible beauty was one of us, was human. And this human lived 30,000 to 50,000 years ago! Our find grows even more mysterious if we take into account the work of innumerable anthropologists who tell us that it was exactly at this time when the human creature as we know him and her today emerged from the night of evolutionary chance into the dazzling light of the beauty seen now before us. Moreover, this period is memorable for what John Pfeiffer, the noted anthropologist, called the "creative explosion," the profusion of works of art that marks what is known as the Upper Paleolithic Age.[3] When the human creature entered this stage of history, he and she did so with a bang. And he and she did so with apparently religious reasons.

As Pfeiffer observes, the art that is found in caves such as Lascaux is "deep art," that is, "art located in utter darkness, far from daylight and twilight zones and living places, on wide expanses of wall or doubly hidden inside tiny chambers, caves within caves, secrets within secrets. . . . It suggests such things as intense rituals, ordeals, journeys underground for mystical reasons."[4] The cave of Lascaux fits this description perfectly. Immediately inside the entrance is a great hall, or nave, known as the "Hall of Bulls" for its display of four enormous black aurochs bulls. This hall extends into what is known as the "Passage," a long (about 45 feet) and narrow (6 to 12 feet wide) stretch whose walls bear over 400 engravings. Off to one side in the "Passage" is a basilica-like structure known as the "Great Apse." This apse literally explodes with art, with over 1,000 engravings and with almost half of them being some sort of abstract sign. A liturgist might exclaim that if this were a church, the "Great Apse" would correspond to a particularly sacred place of ritual. That suspicion seems affirmed, for within the "Great Apse" there lies a very special place in this stone temple. It is known as the crypt or shaft and is believed to be the "holy of holies" of this most ancient church. On its dome-like roof, like an Eastern icon, is an amazing painting. A "wounded hunter" with a birdlike head lies at the feet of an equally wounded bison eviscerated by what appears to be the spear of the hunter. Though some dismiss it as the depiction of a hunting accident, most serious scholars see this painting depicting a shaman, a holy man, lying in a trance evidently trying to unite with the spirit of the bison.[5] The interlacing of religion and art at this moment in time when our first human ancestors entered the evolutionary stage suggests that religion is a fundamental dimension of art and that art is a fundamental dimension of our humanity.

The Transcendentals

Lascaux suggests that art and religion appear to have the same roots. Most theologians would go even further: God is beauty. And the beautiful is the medium par excellence by which we experience the love and knowledge of God. A look around some contemporary churches, however, reveals few works of art of recent origin. Church after church interior presents a visual silence of stark function and hospital-like economy. Given the close connection between God and the beautiful, one can only ask: Why have the arts fared so poorly in the churches of our day? Where are our cathedral craftsmen, our Michelangelos, Berninis, and Donatellos? Indeed, what has happened to this ancient relationship between religion and art? One can ask, perhaps, an even more disturbing question: *What has happened to the beautiful, not only in the church, but, also, in our society?* . . .

An answer might be found in M. Clottes' response. What is most amazing about the Stone Age cave paintings is not the fact of their great age, but that after scores of millennia, these ancient paintings still move another human being to tears. The cave paintings at Lascaux demonstrate a truth our world seems to have forgotten. There exist values that transcend space and time. There exist realities that pervade the entire universe either through the vast reaches of unimaginable light-years of space or the vast journeys of unimaginable eons of time. There exist presences that allow us an intimacy with God.

Theologians and philosophers have long spoken of these values, presences, and realities. These are the "transcendentals": the true, the good, and the beautiful.[6] The transcendentals provide a key in understanding a theological paradox. How can a finite human creature experience or even speak of the infinite God? How can the finite human creature name the nameless, perceive the imperceptible, make visible the invisible? In the past, theologians have answered these questions through the transcendentals. Because God is truth, goodness, even beauty itself, an experience of truth, goodness, or beauty is also an experience of intimacy with God. Because we depend on God for our very existence, we also depend on our experience of truth, goodness, and beauty for our very lives. Irenaeus, the great theologian of the second century, exquisitely phrased it: "The glory of the Lord is living human being, and human being lives for the vision of God." Irenaeus tells us that we were made to see God, our very life depends on seeing God, and thus in a sense our very lives depend on seeing truth, goodness, and beauty.

If Irenaeus is correct, then we are in deep, deep trouble. The transcendentals, you see, have fallen on hard times. The dearth of works of beauty in our churches is but one example. When was the last time you heard someone speak of truth? When was the last time you heard someone speak of the common good? The human horrors of the twentieth century, the lingering nightmares of two world wars, a cold war threatening unbelievable destruction, and the heartlessness of ethnic cleansing, have shaken our confidence in the true, the good, and the beautiful as intrinsic to our humanity, indeed, to the entire creation. This pervasive lack of conviction in presences, values, and realities that transcend our particular lives and histories is the reason I mentioned that theologians refer to the transcendentals in the past sense. Many theologians, I'm afraid, have also lost their confidence in truth, goodness, and the beautiful. Not all theologians have, however. Among these theologians, one stands out for an impressive sustained theological reflection on the transcendentals.[7]

The late Hans Urs von Balthasar, a Swiss theologian and former Jesuit, felt that the loss of the transcendentals in theological reflection threatened theology itself. As he put it: "No longer loved or fostered by religion, beauty is lifted from its face as a mask, and its absence exposes features on that face which threaten to become incomprehensible to man. We no longer dare to believe in beauty and we make of it a mere appearance in order the more easily to dispose of it. . . . We can be sure that whoever sneers at her name as if she were the ornament of a bourgeois past—whether he admits it or not—can no longer pray and soon will no longer be able to love."[8] Indeed, von Balthasar offered a theological aesthetics to bring back theologians to reflection on the beautiful. Von Balthasar, however, did not give us much by the way of a theology of art.

As such, it is regrettable. A theological aesthetics without a theology of art is not able in itself to address the problem of the loss of beauty von Balthasar raises.[9] Yes, we must learn to find beauty once again or we will find ourselves in a world "no longer able to love": But how is beauty once more to be found? It would do no good to simply say, "Look and see, beauty is all around you." For that is the problem. We have forgotten how to look and see. That is where a theology of art comes in. It is art, I believe, that promises to teach theology how to see again.

Unfortunately, art itself seems to be in a crisis. It, too, has forgotten its service to beauty. Many philosophers of art and art critics have lost conviction that art has any connection to the beautiful. Art has become, instead, a self-conscious dialogue with itself. To understand a contemporary piece of art, one must also understand the recent history of that art. In other words, art has become more a self-conscious dialogue with its own history than the discovery of the beautiful. Indeed, a growing number of philosophers, art critics, and even artists have sounded an alarm.[10]

There are two major reasons, I believe, for this crisis. One is art's loss of reference to its theological dimension. Art's theological dimension has its origin in God's own art, the natural beauty of Creation. Indeed, the human participates in that natural beauty by virtue of being one of God's creatures. The human creature, however, participates in God's art in another way. He and she are able to contemplate it. In doing so, the human creature catches an intriguing and wondrous glimpse of itself. In the beauty of God's work, we catch a glimpse of our own beauty. Beauty, natural or the work of human hands, has an intrinsic reference to the mystery of our own creatureliness. For various reasons, our age appears to reject or ignore this wondrous reference in its artistic expressiveness.

The other reason for the crisis in art is that our age has forgotten that the experience of Beauty, that is, the beautiful, is a complex, intrinsically communal experience that cannot be easily categorized. The beautiful has to do with what moves the heart and thus the grotesque and unattractive can also manifest beauty. Moreover, the beautiful is discerned not as a dyadic, private experience between an individual and a work of art but as a triadic experience that is intrinsically communal.[11] But to see the beauty in the grotesque and unattractive, one must engage the communal dimension of beauty. In this sense, art needs theology. For theology can discern the beautiful in the agonized face of a crucified man not as a sadistic exercise or as an expression of deep despair but because theology recognizes that Beauty shines through the suffering in this world through its communal dimension. Theology discerns the beautiful in the face of a crucified man through the lens of the community that gathers around the foot of his cross. Indeed, it is the communal dimension of art that allows the beautiful to shine through the most tragic depiction of the human condition. Without the communal dimension of art, artistic depictions of suffering lend themselves to despair or cynicism, or worse, sadism.

Given these two sides of a crisis, the crisis of the loss of conviction that the beautiful exists, the call for a theology of art seems to me inescapable. Art needs theology and theology needs art. Theology needs art because art teaches theology to "see." And art needs theology because theology not only can guide and encourage art to look for the beautiful in the depths of the human mystery but can also help art regain its communal dimension through which the beautiful shines through the violence and pain of this troubled world. As such, theology can help art reach its full potential. But what would such a theology of art look like?

Theology and Art

John Dillenberger, in his marvelous book *A Theology of Artistic Sensibilities*, tackles the difficult problem of the proper relationship between theology and art. Dillenberger suggests three contemporary approaches that propose a relationship between theology and art.[12] The first approach, he calls, "the divorce between theology and art."[13] This approach sees a negative relationship between theology and art. Exemplifying this approach are Rudolph Bultmann and Karl Barth. Though Barth was quite public in his appreciation of Mozart, he nonetheless vehemently opposed placing stained glass in the Basel Minster. He once wrote that images and symbols "have no place at all in a building designed for Protestant worship."[14] The second approach Dillenberger calls "Affirmations of a Relation between Art and Theology." This approach sees a positive relationship between theology and art. Exemplifying this approach is George Lindbeck and Paul Tillich. In *The Nature of Doctrine*, Lindbeck, for example, attempts to understand how different doctrines can yet find a deeper unity. Lindbeck points out that Grünewald's *Crucifixion* and the Byzantine *Pantocrator* are united in the subject they depict yet the images represent different historical experiences of that subject. For Lindbeck, "the aesthetic and nondiscursively symbolic dimensions of a religion—for example its poetry, music, art and rituals" are not simply ornaments but effective expressions of the religion itself.[15]

Finally, the third approach, Dillenberger calls "The Arts as Models for Theological Work." Similar to the second approach, it posits a positive but more intimate relationship between theology and art. Exemplifying this approach are Hans Urs von Balthasar and Karl Rahner. Rahner puts it,

> insofar as theology is man's reflexive self-expression about himself in the light of divine revelation, we could propose the thesis that theology cannot be complete until it appropriates these arts as an integral moment of itself and its own life, until the arts become an intrinsic moment of theology itself. One could take the position that what comes to expression in a Rembrandt painting or a Bruckner symphony is so inspired and borne by divine revelation, by grace and by God's self-communication, that they communicate something about what the human really is in the eyes of God which cannot be completely translated into verbal theology. . . . If theology is simply and arbitrarily defined as being identical with verbal theology, then of course we cannot say that. But then we would have to ask whether such a reduction of theology to verbal theology does justice to the value and uniqueness of these arts, and whether it does not unjustifiably limit the capacity of the arts to be used by God in his revelation.[16]

Dillenberger, however, is not happy with any of these approaches. He agrees with Karl Rahner's observation above that "the arts cannot be translated entirely into other modalities, but that what they uniquely disclose must nevertheless have implications for theological work."[17] Dillenberger agrees that the relationship between theology and art is positive but, realistically, it is also at times problematic. Dillenberger is anxious to allow both theology and art their own methods independent of each other, but he warns that attempting to find too close a unity between theology and the arts is ultimately frustrating. For art has its own discipline unique to itself, and interdisciplinary as theology can be, it needs to be aware of the unique modality that is art.[18] He believes the relationship between theology and art ought to be one that is positive but pluralistic in nature. As he puts it,

> We live in a pluralistic world, a world with many convictions and many sensibilities. For some, that may be incapacitating. For others, an understanding of this diversity may also be a new opportunity, a way of understanding cultural diversity as also an expression of a split within humanity. Because our sensibilities are diverse, each offering something the other does not even when it centers on the same reality, we have the choice of taking one at the expense of the others or of counting on all of them even when we know that we will not be able to cultivate all in equal ways. There is a division in our very nature, an affinity with a difference among our sensibilities—sight, touch, taste, hearing, speaking. These modalities, understood from the point of creation, define our full humanity in relation to God. Understood from the standpoint of our actual state—from the perspective of the fall, if you will—the unity does not come

> naturally. Understood from the point of redemption, we need the discipline of each sensibility in order to express a full humanity eschatologically oriented to its fulfillment.[19]

In other words, Dillenberger recognizes that the intersection between theology and art is often haphazard. A smooth relationship between theology and art does not come easily. He explains this haphazard relationship as due to the difference between fallen and redeemed sensibilities. This side of paradise, human beings fail. We experience dichotomies where there should be unity. Someday, in the Final Times, human beings shall experience the kind of unity sensed in our best moments, but for now we must learn to live with the disunity that is the lot of the human condition. For this reason, there is need for a separate discipline of art and a separate discipline of theology to guide our human fallibility. Nonetheless, he believes, from the point of view of the Final Times, theology and art do have a mysterious unity. This tension between fallen and redeemed sensibilities is the proper relationship between theology and art.

I find Dillenberger's proposal compelling. His distinction between fallen and redeemed sensibilities closely resonates with elements of Roman Catholic tradition. I would differ with him, however, in the emphasis one places in the separation between fallen and redeemed sensibilities. Roman Catholic tradition is more optimistic about the nature of that separation. Roman Catholic theology would see continuity rather than sharp separation. This belief in continuity suggests that the failure at times for art to engage theology is not simply the result of a fundamental human alienation but, perhaps, the loss of a spiritual dimension.[20] This loss is symptomatic of human alienation but not disastrously so. As such, there exists a range of possibilities for art to engage theology. The theologian could then affirm that even though all art, ultimately, has a religious dimension not all art participates effectively in that dimension. In other words, there exist norms by which the religious dimension of a work of art can be explored.

I believe, nonetheless, that Dillenberger is quite correct when he suggests that the relationship between theology and art might be analogous to the relationship between fallen and redeemed sensibilities. Roman Catholic tradition, as we shall see, gives Dillenberger's proposal much support. Dillenberger's proposal is even more compelling in the light of the implications the Lascaux cave paintings have for the relationship between theology and art.

Fallen and Redeemed Sensibilities

Lascaux resonates with Dillenberger's distinction between fallen and redeemed sensibilities for various reasons. After all, the evolutionary emergence of the human creature coincides with Christian beliefs in the origins of the human creature. If the "creative explosion" marks the beginning of a new species, the human upon this earth, it also refers to the time mentioned in the book of Genesis when Adam and Eve were created in the image of God. The Lascaux paintings may tell us some Bible story of Paradise, our first parents, and even the Fall. This does not mean that Lascaux is the site of Paradise. (I suspect that the place of Paradise and the Fall is found in the human heart). Nonetheless, the paintings of Lascaux will also reveal something to us about the makeup of our humanity as it first begins its tragic journey in this world.

Dillenberger's distinction between fallen and redeemed sensibilities also strikes a Roman Catholic chord. There is a long tradition beginning with Origen on the distinction between the physical senses and the spiritual senses.[21] Origen suggests that in the Fall what had been an "original and richly abundant capacity to perceive God" through the five senses degenerated into a lower, material set of five senses with a higher, but greatly diminished, corresponding spiritual set of five senses. Fallen humanity still retains the spiritual senses but now they are diminished and not in harmonious union with the physical senses. Nonetheless, there are times when these two senses become one and a wondrous reality delights the blessed man or woman who experiences this rare but not impossible union. Von Balthasar argued that there is both an ordinary and a mystical dimension to experienced reality. Von Balthasar believed that in the union of the physical and spiritual senses the mystical dimension of everyday reality opened up for us. When people report smelling "roses" instead of the stink of death at the site of the death of a beloved saint, it is this union of the physical and the spiritual senses and the opening up of the mystical within the ordinary that takes place. Perhaps less esoteric, the mystical dimension of reality is analogous to the experience of all art that turns everyday realities into the experience of an extraordinary reality.

The great Roman Catholic philosopher of the arts, Jacques Maritain, articulated another type of theological speculation that involves the union of a fallen and redeemed dimension of the human creature. In his classic essay *Art and Scholasticism*, Maritain reasoned that delight in beauty is a human experience where intuition and intelligence become one. Experience of the beautiful, Maritain explains, is the union of the intuition of the senses and the pure intelligence of the intellect. It is, he observed, what is left for us of Paradise. This is how Adam and Eve must have seen the world before the Fall. As he put it:

> Beauty is essentially the object of intelligence, for what knows in the full meaning of the word is the mind, which alone is open to the infinity of being. The natural site of beauty is the intelligible world: thence it descends. But it also falls in a way within the grasp of the senses, since the senses in the case of man serve the mind and can themselves rejoice in knowing. . . . The part played by the senses in the perception of beauty becomes in our case enormous and well-nigh indispensable, because our mind is not intuitive like the angelic mind; it can perceive, no doubt, but only on condition of abstracting and discoursing. In man only intuivity is necessary for the perception of the beautiful. So also man can certainly enjoy purely intelligible beauty, but the beautiful which is connatural to man is that which comes to delight the mind through the senses and their intuition. Such also is the peculiar beauty of our art, which works upon a sensible matter for the joy of the spirit. It would fain so persuade itself that paradise is not lost. It has the savour of the terrestrial paradise, because it restores for a brief moment the simultaneous peace and delight of the mind and the senses.[22]

Like the split between the physical and spiritual senses, Roman Catholic Scholastic tradition observed in fallen humanity a split between intuition and the intellect. In the beauty manifested through a work of art, however, the sensible and the intelligible become one. Indeed, Maritain goes on to say that such a union of sense and intellect was probably the way Adam and Eve experienced the world around them. What is more provocative, however, is his contention that such a union is still possible for us on this side of the Fall! In other words, Maritain reflects a Roman Catholic emphasis not only on the distinction between fallen and redeemed humanity but also on the continuity between an innocent and a fallen humanity.

Because of these traditions, a Roman Catholic theology of art would add a refinement to Dillenberger's dual proposal for a positive relationship between theology and art and the need to keep distinct the methods and subject matter of theology and art. The Catholic emphasis on continuity between our original and fallen states suggests that the relationship between theology and art is more intimate than any of the approaches so far mentioned by Dillenberger. The intimacy of this relationship, however, is not one where theology and art are simply flip sides of the same coin. Nor is the intimacy between theology and art one in which they share the same methods. Rather, the fallen and redeemed sensibilities are parts of a continuum of human experience that is available to us on this side of Paradise. A Roman Catholic theology of art would be one that explores this continuum giving an account of how theology and art relate to one another.

For this to happen, however, Roman Catholic theology needs help from a philosophy capable of exploring the continuity of experience. The closest philosophical tradition at Roman Catholic theology's disposal is the Scholastic philosophical tradition. Unfortunately, that tradition has fallen on hard times and it would be almost anachronistic to introduce it as a serious partner for a theology of art. There is, however, a philosophical tradition that builds upon the Scholastic tradition and has, as its maxim, the continuity of experience. This is the North American philosophical tradition that began with Charles S. Peirce and was developed by Josiah Royce, and also John Dewey.[23] Though I will not be spelling out this philosophical tradition in detail, the subsequent chapters are a sympathetic application of their insights in these sketches toward a theology of art.[24]

One more element, however, is missing. The distinction between fallen and redeemed sensibilities presupposes the existence of evil or, more appropriately, the human experience of suffering. A theology of art that cannot give account of beauty from within the garden of good and evil fails to convince as theology. And art that cannot see beauty in the midst of the evil that exists in the world is not worthy of its high calling. The existence of evil, however, makes problematic a theology of art that does not question contemporary understandings of the beautiful. How can one speak of the beautiful in light of the terrible suffering that exists in the world? How can one support the luxury of art when so many are in need of basics such as food, shelter, and clothing? Here too, the North American philosophical tradition offers some help through the insights of Josiah Royce. Royce took the problem of evil quite seriously and, in applying Charles Peirce's social insights into logic to the question of theodicy, he brought the Scholastic tradition much closer to contemporary concerns. Moreover, I have argued in *Community of the Beautiful* that our understanding of the beautiful needs much rethinking. The beautiful is not necessarily the "pretty" or the "pleasing." I believe the beautiful is not simply a quality that is self-evident or a judgment of taste but a reality, indeed, a community, being discovered and evolving. Here, too, Lascaux offers some suggestions.

Art from within the Garden of Good and Evil

Perhaps the greatest lesson to be learned at Lascaux is what truly marks a creature as human. A long philosophical and scientific tradition marks the rise of the truly human with the rise of the rational mind or self-consciousness. A newer, more cynical tradition from the psychological sciences, however, marks the rise of the human with brutal violence. This tradition sees our humanity emerging from its animal roots in a brutal, calculated act of violence that would be the first murder.[25] The violence depicted in the disembowelment of the bison gives reason to believe that the latter tradition is true.

Lascaux, on the other hand, offers a surprisingly different perspective: The mark of our humanity lies in works of beauty. That humans are rational may be questioned and violence mainly points out our inhumanity but there's no doubt that works of art mark that human presence. Indeed, what we find at the origins of humanity are not books of philosophy or murderous bands of savages but artists capable of incredible works of beauty.

A gaze at the lines that reveal the bison forms shows something more than intelligence or violence at work. Such lines reveal a disciplined freedom, a gracefulness that is more than the work of a self-conscious mind. They are an epiphany of the human soul. Indeed, these graced curves of the bison reveal a mysterious and marvelous union of sensibility and creativity that guided a human soul to shape a set of lines that still evoke, even 30,000 years later, a sense of childlike wonder, and yes, beauty. We have labeled these first artists "primitive," suggesting their minds were not as developed as ours. Yet if intelligence is to be measured by its beauty, then these first artists may have been more intelligent than we who live today with little to show by way of the intelligence of beauty.

Likewise, those who emphasize the violence depicted, such as the one found in the painting known as the "wounded hunter," miss the profound religious significance of the painting. Yes, it portrays violence, a bison disemboweled by a hunter. But the beauty of the painting lies not in the celebration of such violence. The "wounded hunter" does not see violence as something to be celebrated. As mentioned earlier, most serious scholars see this painting as depicting a shaman, a holy man, lying in a trance evidently trying to unite with the spirit of the bison. Some see this painting depicting a profound compassion. It is as if the pain of the bison speared in the hunt moves the shaman, who, forgetting his own safety, goes into a trance in order to undergo a dangerous spiritual journey of compassion in hopes of uniting with the bison spirit. Such a union taking place, the shaman would then console and give thanks to the bison for its life.

Some scholars, on the other hand, see the "wounded hunter" as portraying a profound sense of intercession. In taking the bison's life, the shaman asks the bison not to take revenge for the taking of the bison's life but for sympathy with the need of the shaman's community to live. Three elements appear to be at work here. One is a profound sense of the unity and interconnectedness of life. The first humans recognized that their lives depended on the life of the bison. The hunter lived because the hunted also lived. More interestingly, the wounded hunter depicts the ability of humans to transcend identity of self and identify with another. This capacity for what Joseph Campbell calls a "transpersonal identity" lies at the heart of religious experience and also, it appears, of art. The ability to put oneself in place of another or, in the case of the artist, in place of the work of art, is a profound human act. Moreover, it is an act of compassion. The wounded hunter depicts less a savage humanity than a profound compassion, an extraordinary human act of transpersonal identification with the life that must be given so that the hunter too can live.

The other element of the Lascaux religious experience is a great sense of vulnerability. Such vulnerability is both an acknowledgement of a spiritual limitation and an openness for that limitation to be transcended. Such openness is sympathy in the sense that it is empathy "in reverse." It is a call to the sacred to act upon the one seeking it. Indeed, there is an awesome sympathy at work in the religious experience of the sacred. In other words, religious vulnerability is an openness that is intercessory in nature. It is the religious experience of sympathy. And it is an experience that lends itself to art. Art becomes a "bridge" to the sacred through the evoking of compassion and the call for divine sympathy. Compassion and sympathy become the twin suspension lines of a religious aesthetic bridge that unites the human with the sacred.

There is, finally, a third element in the religious experience that is Lascaux. It is a great sense of awe and wonder at the beauty of the bison. But what provokes this wonder? A clue to an answer to this question is the observation that the "wounded hunter" was meant to be seen in the deepest and darkest part of the cave where sounds take on an eerie, mystical quality and torchlight brings forth spirit-like shadows. In this atmosphere, the "wounded hunter" gives rise to marvelous wonder in its beautiful, graced lines. But "atmosphere" seems an unlikely answer to our question. I believe, rather, that the answer lies in examining that which provoked the same wonder in M. Clottes.

M. Clottes recognized something remarkably akin to his own humanity in the paintings of Lascaux. Indeed, Clottes recognized something that pointed to his own humanity residing within the beauty of the bison. Thus, I suspect that the position of the "wounded hunter" in the dark depths of the cave was less an attempt to provide an "atmosphere" than to encourage the beholder to contemplate the beauty of the bison in the dark depths of one's own heart.[26] The wonder felt by Clottes and the beholder of the "wounded hunter" was, I believe, the result of an experience of deep recognition that in the beauty of these animals was a glimmer of what it truly means to be human.

Such wonder must have been even more profound for our ancestors for it is provoked from within the garden of good and evil. It is a wonder achieved in spite of the violence that surrounds it. Indeed, it is even more wondrous because of it. Imagine, if you will, killing that which you find most beautiful. Add to that the realization that you kill not out of hate but that one may live. Then one can see the great paradox that must have faced our first parents. As such, the bond between the beauty of the bison and the human beholder appears to be found in the woundedness of both the bison and the hunter. The bison is wounded but so is the hunter for he has killed that which he loves. Thus there exists a mysterious bond in this woundedness that is the key to our wonder. For wonder achieved from within an environment of violence and suffering, emerging out a mysterious woundedness that binds two creatures, reflects extraordinary human abilities, abilities hinted at in the beauty of the painting of the bison.

Indeed, the religious experience of Lascaux illumines the nature of the beautiful and the human capacity for making works of beauty. The human making of works of beauty speaks of an extraordinary ability that emerges from the very essence of our humanity. Lascaux suggests that the artistic impulse arises from a profound wonder emerging, begun with a glimpse into the origins of our own beauty and culminating in a woundedness that offers a profound glimpse into our own humanity. Such wonder is a mixture of woundedness and strength, calls for sympathy and acts of compassion. It is a vision from the garden of good and evil describing what theology would call the "beautiful." And such wonder is, at its most profound, a type of innocence, a wounded innocence that opens up the depths of human dignity.

A Wounded Innocence

The paintings of Lascaux reveal a marvelous human dignity. Yet, I believe that today few are convinced that such human dignity exists. If the modern era began with a celebration of the human person, the Renaissance, then it is ending with an almost cynical conviction in an insuperable violence, deceit, and cruelty woven deep into the human fabric. The wise architects of Vatican II responded to this widespread cynicism by emphasizing the dignity of the human person. This emphasis, however, continues to fall on deaf ears. The task of theology as I see it, in responding to this unfortunate attitude, is not one of reminding society of the worth of the human person. Rather, the task is one of learning how to "see" again the dignity of the human person. And part of that learning to "see" again the dignity of the human person is learning to "see" again that marvelous innocence that is the depth of the dignity of the human person.

Part of the problem in "seeing" once again the innocence of the human person is the reduction in meaning of innocence. A great part of our understanding of innocence has been shaped by the legal system and a moral philosophy that can be traced back to Kant and the Enlightenment. A certain "conceit" of moral philosophers is that experience is permanently corrupting.[27] This does not mean that innocence then is a noble trait. Rather, innocence is the mark of moral immaturity, a type of a "pre-reflective, natural state." As Alexander Eodice puts it, "though experience corrupts, knowledge resolves the problem of ignorance." Thus, innocence is also a mark of moral immaturity because it is also seen as a kind of ignorance. This "conceit" sees innocence not only as the opposite of experience but also as a type of ignorance. Such a view has terrible consequences for a positive, theological view of art that sees art as somehow redemptive. Art involves both the element of experience and a special kind of intelligence. Given the above understanding of experience, it is hard to find something redemptive not only in innocence but also in art.

Part of the problem is that the above view of innocence combines two very different senses of innocence that ought to be distinguished. There is innocence with respect to actions but there also is a sense of innocence as it describes the state of a person. Innocence with respect to actions lends itself to legal language and concepts. The ordinary sense of this type of innocence is that someone is absolved of being guilty of committing some terrible deed. Innocence as describing a human condition, however, lends itself to theological language. Such innocence describes the nature or character of a person. Unfortunately, this type of innocence is very hard to describe.

Many describe this type of innocence in terms of "lacks"—the lack of self-critical ability, the lack of knowledge, and so on.[28] As such, innocence is really describing the innocence of a child. It is an innocence that describes a certain kind of moral purity. No wonder, then, that so many horror movies feature evil in a child. Evil in a child is horrific precisely because the child represents a kind of innocence that is synonymous with moral purity. What is more difficult to understand is the kind of innocence that would apply to an adult. Evil in an adult no longer seems to shock us. It is expected, even prescribed by many. Yet how can the horror of evil be recognized, even judged, without the presence of some innocence in the human person. Part of this loss of conviction in the innocence of an adult is due to this equivalence between innocence and moral purity. I agree that innocence, as moral purity, is impossible in an adult. But there is another kind of innocence possible.

This type of innocence is capable of exciting wonder in us. It can be recognized as something beautiful and "particularly rare and wonderful." Indeed, I will argue that this type of innocence is the stuff of which the beautiful is made. It is innocence, Eodice tells us, seen as a virtue, innocence seen as something to be achieved. In the language of ontology, such innocence is a "radical openness to being more." Such innocence is the opposite of ignorance for it relies on knowledge to achieve its state. Moreover, the type of innocence an adult is capable of having is not an innocence free from guilt. Thus, Eodice tells us, this innocence is "the difference between a person who feels guilt and . . . one who chooses to redeem himself through internal suffering."[29] This type of innocence is only possible through the requirement of love. Love, as the great philosopher Ludwig Wittgenstein puts it, is that which is needed by "my heart, my soul, not my speculative intelligence."[30] Wittgenstein, it may surprise many, has to say a lot about this kind of innocence. Elizabeth Wolgast in her article "Innocence," notes an important distinction by Wittgenstein. Wittgenstein distinguished between innocence as the natural absence of temptation and innocence as something a person has fought to achieve.[31]

In theology, the understanding of innocence emerges, in part, from interpretations of the biblical story of Adam and Eve. This understanding of innocence is both negative and static. Before the Fall, Adam and Eve live in a state of innocence. Innocence as a state is also innocence seen as static. Adam and Eve then lose their innocence. This is a negative view of innocence. Innocence is not described, we know of it only because it is lost. This negative view of innocence means that innocence, if it is to be positively understood, must be associated with something more familiar. One association sees Adam and Eve in Paradise as existing in a state of both innocence and ignorance. The forbidden fruit promises to remedy their ignorance with the "knowledge of good and evil." Indeed, the possibility to know as God knows appears to be the most human temptation of all. Falling into temptation, Adam and Eve eat the forbidden fruit which remedies the lack of ignorance but also results in the total loss of innocence.

Another association sees Adam and Eve in Paradise as existing in a state of both innocence and not having yet committed any moral (or immoral) acts. Eating the forbidden fruit proves to be the first act they make with moral consequences. As such, it is an immoral act and the shame of their nakedness points to the nature of the immorality. Thus, innocence is seen as previous to moral action. In both of these associations, innocence is known negatively and statically. In terms of the transcendentals, it associates innocence negatively with the True, (ignorance) or with the Good (lack of moral action). Such a negative and static understanding of human innocence tends to be ambivalent about the possibility of human self-transcendence. In its worst implications, it is, in part, responsible for the tragic debates and misunderstandings of the nature of justification in the Reformation.

Eodice, Wolgast, and Wittgenstein provide the theologian with a means to challenge these associations. There is a dynamic dimension to human innocence that has been neglected in the theological tradition. Neglected but not unknown, that is, for there is a great patristic interpretation that suggests this dynamic understanding of innocence. I am speaking of that ancient understanding of the Adam and Eve story found in the writings of Irenaeus. Irenaeus sees the Adam and Eve story as less a tale of the Fall than a tale of expulsion and subsequent pilgrimage. The expulsion from Paradise begins a journey of both learning and moral advancement.

It is a tale of an exile that becomes a pilgrimage to an elevated humanity rather than a tale of guilt and shame. It is a tale of redemption rather than punishment. Henri Rondet captures this tradition when he tells us that "Man as visualized by Irenaeus is, on the contrary, a young being, looking to the future; the evils—even sins—of life are but growing pains. Paradise, in a way, is less in the past than in the future, indeed, ever-present as a step to that future. The history of man is not that of a laborious ascent after a vertical fall, but a providential progress towards a future that is full of promise."[32] It is this kind of interpretation that allows a theology of art to take root and flourish. Indeed, it is a story of an innocence that is to be achieved. It is the story of an innocence that is a "radical openness to being more." Since the nature of the beautiful is also about "being more," it is an understanding of innocence that has potential of being associated with the third transcendental.

The biblical story of Adam and Eve interpreted through the eyes of the Irenaean tradition also speaks of a certain woundedness in the human condition, a poignant vulnerability. One can get hurt on the way to Paradise. Yet such vulnerability is a condition to reach Paradise. Indeed, the Fall has been interpreted in the liturgy as a *felix culpa,* a "happy fault." The Fall brought to self-consciousness a profound vulnerability, a radical openness to being acted upon, that, ultimately, expresses itself as the need for intercession, a call for sacred sympathy. As such, the *felix culpa* tradition becomes what Josiah Royce called a "religious insight," an insight into the need and way of salvation.[33]

As religious insight, sacred sympathy plays a divine role in our human journey. It becomes a means through which we can interpret our humanity. Sacred sympathy finds its ultimate manifestation in the Incarnation. The Incarnation, indeed, is a crucial element in a theology of art. The Incarnation, through Irenaean eyes, however, adds a new dimension to a theology of art and to a theological understanding of innocence.

If the Irenaean tradition is applied to the meaning of the Incarnation, Jesus appears not only as divine Redeemer but also human Rabbi. As Rabbi, Jesus is inspired teacher. As Teacher and Redeemer, Jesus teaches us what it means to be truly human. As Teacher and Redeemer, however, Jesus also "lifts off the veil" of the meaning of our humanity.[34] Jesus offers an "interpretant," an "apocalyptic" to our humanity. Jesus is the Lamb of God, the Innocent One, and in this Innocence we find, as well, the meaning of our innocence, our humanity, and our salvation.

The Incarnation offers an eschatological dimension best seen through the eyes of Irenaeus. That eschatological dimension inspired this constructive attempt to a theology of art. As such, this book suggests that, in a profound sense, the theological dimension of art lies in that, ultimately, art interprets humanity to the human. Interpreting humanity to the human calls for a special kind of "interpretant," a guide not only to human understanding but also human transformation. This human transformation participates as an eschatological sign of the Incarnation. For it interprets humanity to the human in the context of the garden of good and evil. In a sense, art redeems the motivation for eating the forbidden fruit. Art, at its religious best, transforms a disobedient arrogance into *a wounded innocence.*

Thus, the Incarnation becomes the foundation of a theology of art. Given the insights of the Irenaean tradition, however, the eschatological dimension of the Incarnation suggests a little explored possibility for a theology of art, the dynamics of an innocence emerging from human struggle within the garden of good and evil. As such, this theology of art is a story of exile and pilgrimage, of human compassion and divine sympathy. It is the story of the Incarnation not only as God-with-us but also as heaven-with-us. It is a story of the struggle to understand our very humanity from within the garden of good and evil. It is a story of the redemptive power of that struggle, a struggle for an innocence to be achieved. And in the achieving of that innocence, a certain human participation in the atoning of the world's sins takes place. Indeed, it is a story about justification and sanctification. It is a story about learning how to be fully human, about learning to fully "see" again, about the reuniting of the fallen and redeemed sensibilities to see the truly beautiful. It is a story about openness to "being more" as well as "being acted upon." Indeed, it is a story about a wondrous openness to the possibilities of the human future. It is a story about a new Christian humanism that opens up the depths of a marvelous human dignity. Indeed, it is a story about theology and art. It is the story of *a wounded innocence.*

1. Monsieur Jean Clottes as quoted in Bruce Crumley, "Archaeology: Cave Art in France," *Time* 145, no. 5 (30 January 1995).

2. Joseph Campbell, *Part 2: Mythologies of the Great Hunt*, vol. 1. The way of the animal powers of *Historical Atlas of World Mythology* (New York: Harper & Row, 1988) xviii.

3. John E. Pfeiffer, *The Creative Explosion: An Inquiry into the Origins of Art and Religion* (New York: Harper & Row, 1982).

4. Ibid., 12.

5. Joseph Campbell, *Part 1: Primitive Hunters and Gatherers*, vol. 1. The way of the animal powers of *Historical Atlas of World Mythology* (New York: Harper & Row, 1988) 65.

6. The transcendentals are discussed in the field of ontology, the study of being. They are, in a sense, a special type of universal. The *transcendentals* are said to be attributes of Being, the One, the True, the Good, and the Beautiful, and are called transcendentals because they are coextensive with Being even as they transcend any one creature. Actually, the history of the philosophy of transcendentals is a long and complicated one (much too long to do it justice in a footnote). At stake in the philosophical debate over the transcendentals is the interconnectedness of reality. What does an

onion have in common with a star? Without a theory of transcendentals, the answer is nothing. With a theory of transcendentals one can say that both the onion and the star are beautiful, good, and true (to their reality). Perhaps the value of the transcendentals is best seen in the environmental debate. Is humanity inextricably connected to its environment? The transcendentals not only give an affirmative answer but also provide a basis for seeing the universe as an interconnected set of relationships. In short, the transcendentals can help articulate a theology of the environment. As philosophical terms, the transcendentals may seem a bit abstract. Let me suggest, as I did in my *Community of the Beautiful,* that they are best seen as communities. The transcendentals are, in this sense, communities in which all reality participates, that is, communities of the True, the Good, and the Beautiful.

7. Hans Urs von Balthasar wrote a multivolume series of works separated into three parts, each part dealing with one of the transcendentals. Thus, the first part was called *Herrlichkeit* or, in translation, "The Glory of the Lord" which dealt with the beautiful, the second part was *Theodramatik,* or "Theo-Drama" which dealt with the Good, and the third part was *Theologik,* or, "Theo-Logic," which dealt with Truth.

8. Hans Urs von Balthasar, *Seeing the Form,* vol. 1 of *The Glory of the Lord* (San Francisco/New York: Ignatius Press/Crossroad Publications, 1983) 19.

9. I was one of those theologians moved by von Balthasar's call to a theological aesthetics. I came to realize later, however, that aesthetics addresses only one side of an essentially triadic relationship. The experience of art involves the artist, the beholder, and the work of art itself. This three-way relationship, however, is one in the experience of art. Aesthetics addresses only the relationship between the work of art and the beholder and as such does not do justice to the inextricable three-part relationship that is art. Thus, a theological aesthetics needs to be expanded from its dyadic relationship between beholder and work of art into the triadic experience which includes the artist. Such an expanded theological aesthetics is the stuff of a theology of art. In other words, a theology of art explores the entire triadic structure of art. Thus, a theological aesthetics that does not include a theology of art is incomplete.

10. Among these one can include J. M. Bernstein, *The Fate of Art: Aesthetic Alienation from Kant to Derrida and Adorno,* Literature and Philosophy (University Park, Pa.: Pennsylvania State University Press, 1992); Arthur Coleman Danto, *After the End of Art: Contemporary Art and the Pale of History,* The A. W. Mellon Lectures in the Fine Arts (Princeton, N.J.: Princeton University Press, 1997); Suzi Gablik, *The Reenchantment of Art* (New York, N.Y.: Thames and Hudson, 1991); Jean-Marie Schaeffer, *Art of the Modern Age: Philosophy of Art from Kant to Heidegger,* New French Thought (Princeton, N.J.: Princeton University Press, 2000).

11. I have argued elsewhere that it makes more sense to speak of the transcendentals as communities rather than abstract principles of the mind. I refer the reader to my *The Community of the Beautiful: A Theological Aesthetics* (Collegeville, Minn.: The Liturgical Press).

12. John Dillenberger, *A Theology of Artistic Sensibilities: The Visual Arts and the Church* (New York: Crossroad, 1986).

13. Ibid., 217.

14. Karl Barth, "The Architectural Problem of Protestant Places of Worship," in *The Christian Place of Worship,* edited by Andre Bieler (Edinburgh and London: Oliver and Boyd, 1965) 93, as quoted in Dillenberger, op. cit., 217.

15. Dillenberger, op. cit., 219–24.

16. Karl Rahner, "Theology and the Arts," *Thought* 57 (1982) 24–25, as quoted in Dillenberger, op. cit., 225–26.

17. Dillenberger, op. cit., 228.

18. Ibid., 231–34.

19. Ibid., 248–49.

20. This is the subject of chapter 2, "The End of Art."

21. Both von Balthasar and Rahner give an excellent account of the tradition of the spiritual senses. They also come to two very different interpretations. For von Balthasar's account, the reader might consult Balthasar, op. cit., 301–428. Karl Rahner's account can be found in Karl Rahner, "La Doctrine des 'Sens Spirituels' au Moyen-Age," *Revue d'Ascétique et de Mystique* 14, no. 55 (1933) 263–99. A helpful comparison of their differing interpretations can be found in Stephens Fields, S.J., "Balthasar and Rahner on the Spiritual Senses," *Theological Studies* 57, no. 2 (June 1996) 224–41.

22. Jacques Maritain, *Art and Scholasticism, and The Frontiers of Poetry* (New York: Scribner, 1962) 19.

23. I am privileged to be a part of the Courtney Murray Group which is a group of theologians, philosophers, and graduate students who meet for a whole month every year at Berkeley to discuss the intricacies of the North American philosophical tradition and its relevance to contemporary theology. One of the founders of this group is my colleague and good friend Fr. Don Gelpi, S.J. Fr. Gelpi, in particular, has used the North American philosophical tradition systematically. A good example of applying the North American philosophical tradition to traditional topics in theology can be found in Donald L. Gelpi, *The Gracing of Human Experience: Rethinking the Relationship Between Nature and Grace* (Collegeville, Minn.: The Liturgical Press, 2001).

24. Not even Aquinas could apply an entire philosophical system in a theological work without altering the system and I am no Aquinas. The North American philosophical tradition in this work serves more as inspiration and guide to the theological enterprise than a direct application. Otherwise the theology becomes nothing more than an illustration of the philosophical system. I ask the reader's patience for a brief summary of this important philosophical tradition. I go into some detail on this tradition in chapter 2 where I discuss the theological dimension of art.

25. I am thinking here of René Girard and his influential studies of sacrificial ritual. See, e.g., René Girard, *La Violence et le Sacré* (Paris: B. Grasset, 1972); René Girard, Jean-Michel Oughourlian, and Guy Lefort, *Things Hidden Since the Foundation of the World* (Stanford, Calif.: Stanford University Press, 1987); René Girard, *The Scapegoat* (Baltimore: Johns Hopkins University Press, 1986).

26. Indeed, I believe the entire architecture of the cave parallels an inner spiritual journey that culminates in the contemplation of one's own heart.

27. I am indebted in much of the following argument to Alexander R. Eodice, "Innocence Lost and Found," *American Catholic Philosophical Quarterly* 74, no. 2000 (2001) 299–305.

28. A parallel to this understanding of innocence in the philosophy of art is found in the work of E. H. Gombrich. In his *Art and Illusion,* Gombrich argues against the notion of an "innocent" eye such as the one sought by the Impressionists. The "innocent eye" attempted to be free of any visual presuppositions and tried to see the world as "innocently" as possible. Gombrich argues effectively that all "seeing" involves "knowing," that is, all

art takes part in a history of schemas or tradition. In other words, art has a history and, thus, the "innocent" eye, that is, a "seeing" that has not been "contaminated" by knowing is an illusion. Gombrich's account of the "innocent" eye, however, has its flaws. How does one explain paintings that give an accurate depiction of the world we see? Is it possible to have paintings that give an accurate experience of the visual world without some kind of "innocence"? Can one truly speak of being faithful to the information of experience without some kind of innocence? These questions show the inadequacy of an understanding of innocence as ignorance or a lack of knowing. To truly know something, a certain kind of innocence is needed but it is, admittedly, a mysterious kind of innocence. In any case, Gombrich's work is fundamental for an understanding of art. E. H. Gombrich, *Art and Illusion; a Study in the Psychology of Pictorial Representation,* A. W. Mellon lectures in the fine arts, 1956, Bollingen Series (New York: Pantheon Books, 1961).

29. Eodice, op. cit., 304.

30. Ludwig Wittgenstein, G. H. von Wright, and Heikki Nyman, *Culture and Value,* edited by G. H. von Wright (Chicago: University of Chicago Press, 1980) 33, as quoted in Eodice, op. cit., 304.

31. Elizabet Wolgast, "Innocence," *Philosophy* 68 (1993) 299.

32. Henri Rondet, *Original Sin: The Patristic and Theological Background* (Shannon: Ecclesia Press, 1972) 38. Highly recommended reading on Irenaeus is Mary Ann Donovan, *One Right Reading? A Guide to Irenaeus* (Collegeville, Minn.: The Liturgical Press, 1997).

33. I will have much more to say about religious insight in chapter 2.

34. I am, in a sense, playing with the etymology of the Greek word, ἀποκάλυψις (apocalypsis). Apocalypsis derives from the conjunction of two words, "Apo," which means "taking off," and "kalypto" which means to "uncover." The aesthetic sense of "kalypto," however, is "veil" (*kalymna*). The image it brings to my mind is one from the Song of Songs. The bride dancing before her promised one, removes veil after veil tantalizing her partner with a promised but yet-to-be-seen beauty. The image of unveiling and veiling is a traditional one in theologies of beauty. Its eschatological dimension, however, has not been explored fully Gerhard Friedrich Kittel, ed., "Kalypto," in *Theological Dictionary of the New Testament Abridged in One Volume,* reprint, 1985 (Michigan: Logos Research Systems, Inc., 1995–99).

CHAPTER TWO

The End of Art

Marcel Duchamp's Fountain

Early one morning in April 1917, the American Society of Independent Artists received a package. There was not much excitement in receiving a package from a Mr. R. Mutt. What was exciting was the upcoming exhibition by the Society in which they intended to present all art they received without a jury or any type of screening process. Thus, this package was one of many packages they had received from all sorts of artists in preparation for their first exhibition. Beatrice Wood, a member of the Society, and a close friend of the famous artist Marcel Duchamp, recounts what happened when the package was opened:

> Two days before the Exhibition opened, there was a glistening white object in the storeroom getting readied to be put on the floor. I can remember Walter Arensberg and George Bellows standing in front of it, arguing. Bellows was facing Walter, his body on a menacing slant, his fists doubled, striking at the air in anger. Out of curiosity, I approached.
>
> "We cannot exhibit it," Bellows said hotly, taking out a handkerchief and wiping his forehead.
>
> "We cannot refuse it, the entrance fee has been paid," gently answered Walter.
>
> "It is indecent!" roared Bellows.
>
> "That depends upon the point of view," added Walter, suppressing a grin.
>
> "Someone must have sent it as a joke. It is signed R. Mutt; sounds fishy to me," grumbled Bellows with disgust. Walter approached the object in question and touched its glossy surface. Then with the dignity of a don addressing men at Harvard, he expounded: "A lovely form has been revealed, freed from its functional purpose, therefore a man clearly has made an aesthetic contribution. . . ."
>
> "It is gross, offensive! There is such a thing as decency."
>
> "Only in the eye of the beholder. You forget our bylaws."[1]

They didn't know it yet but the American Society for Independent Artists had encountered what has become the most famous (or rather, infamous) object in the history of art—Marcel Duchamp's "Fountain." *Fountain* was nothing more than an ordinary piece of mass-produced hardware, a urinal, which the British call a "readymade." Duchamp simply took a "readymade" urinal from the showroom of the J. L. Mott Iron Works, rotated it 90 degrees from its ordinary position, and signed it "R. Mutt." To this "creation," he gave the title *Fountain*. Since that initial encounter, *Fountain* has been surrounded by various ironies.

The Society broke their own rules on their very first exhibition and *Fountain* was never exhibited. Indeed, the original *Fountain* has been lost. All we have left is this photograph by the famous photographer Alfred Stieglitz. Meanwhile, this never exhibited, now lost object has become one of the most commented upon pieces in the history of art. William Camfield summarizes this literature succinctly: "Some deny that *Fountain* is art but believe it is significant for the history of art and aesthetics. Others accept it grudgingly as art but deny that it is significant. To complete the circle, some insist *Fountain* is neither art nor an object of historical consequence, while a few assert that *Fountain* is both art and significant—though for utterly incompatible reasons."[2] Whatever *Fountain* is, work of art or not, it not only raises serious question about the nature of art and the art world but also about the role of theology in the arts.

Marcel Duchamp

Marcel Duchamp was a boy in the 1890s surrounded by art and artists. His grandfather was Emile-Frédéric Nicolle, a painter of seascapes and landscapes, and his brothers were the painter Jacques Villon and the sculptor Raymond Duchamp-Villon. Moreover, Marcel lived in a time when France was exploding with new art coming from the likes of Cézanne, Matisse, Picasso, and Braque. It is not a surprise, then, to find Marcel making an early decision to become an artist. As Marcel put it: "When you see so many paintings, you've got to paint." Marcel soon became adept at various styles. He was, however, influenced early on by the Cubists who used to meet at his brother's studio. It didn't take him long to master that style and reveal some of his true spirit, a kind of restlessness that craved novelty. Indeed, in 1964, Duchamp revealed, "painting has always bored me, except at the very beginning, when there was that feeling of opening the eyes to something new."[3]

About this time, Marcel became fascinated by the time lapse photographs of Jules Etienne Moray showing people jumping or running and was inspired to duplicate this motion in space through the Cubist style. What emerged was one of his most famous paintings, *Nude descending a staircase,* of which he made various versions. *Nude descending a staircase* was displayed in February 1913 to the shocked and outraged eyes of visitors to the Armory Show in New York. The headlines of the *New York Times* of Sunday, March 16, 1913, read "Cubists and Futurists are making insanity pay." A cartoon that appeared in *The World* on Monday, February 17, 1913, proclaimed, "Nobody who has been drinking is let in to see this show." It is hard to say what affect such outcry had on Duchamp but it might not be too far off the mark to speculate that he thoroughly enjoyed it.

In any case, Duchamp was becoming more and more impatient with the conventions of art itself, including Cubism. He was struggling as he said to "escape from the prison of tradition." Finally, Duchamp found a way. He took up the technique of mechanical drawing. In this way one "is directed by the impersonality of the ruler" or as he put it: "education is so strong, it holds you like a chain. I didn't get completely free even then, but I tried—I unlearned to draw. I had to forget my *hand*." Duchamp was undergoing a curious transformation. He was distancing himself from his art. He sensed that his freedom and autonomy were compromised even in the act of expressing that freedom by painting directly on the canvas. He could be as free as he liked but the minute his hand made strokes on the canvas, the training and tradition that had created Duchamp the artist revealed themselves. Duchamp found this an unbearable constraint and he began to push this sense of absolute artistic freedom, the freedom of the artist from his art, to the limit.

The opportunity came when he left Paris and arrived in New York. He was already a sort of celebrity with the artist community there after the great outrage over his painting in 1913. Duchamp reveled in the casual and freewheeling life and became bolder. It was here that he began to experiment with "readymades." "Readymades," after all, are exemplary vehicles by which an artist can distance himself from his art. An artist does not have to deal with style or tradition in the "choosing" of a "readymade." There is a type of absolute freedom from the conventions of art in simply being able to "choose" a "readymade" and then declare it to be art. It was this experimentation with "readymades" that culminated in his contribution of *Fountain* to the American Society of Independent Artists.

This brief look at Duchamp's story reveals an artist struggling with the very meaning of art and what it means to be an artist. In that struggle, he distances himself more and more from the subject of his passion until he reaches a point of what he considers to be absolute freedom as an artist. Ironically, he reaches as well a point of almost absolute indifference to art. Is Duchamp's story simply the story of an eccentric genius? Or is there something more fundamental to be found? In a sense, it is both. Duchamp's story is uniquely his own. No one has really succeeded in making "readymades" a kind of artistic style. On the other hand, Duchamp's story, I believe, is a kind of parable about what happens to art when it loses its theological dimension. Moreover, Duchamp's story has not really ended with Duchamp. It is very much alive today and the parable continues to be told in various ways.

Aesthetic Nominalism

Thierry de Duve, in his marvelous book *Nominalisme Pictural*, advances the thesis that "the readymade was a product of the abandonment of art . . . which broke a filial bond [with art] but which also recollected [art's] heritage."[4] Duchamp's "readymade," he says, cannot be held solely responsible for the "abandonment of art" but is the "transition" through which the "nom de peinture," i.e., the name "painting," became detached from its specific method which legitimized it. This passage cannot be the sole work of one man, Duchamp, but the work of an entire culture. Indeed, Duchamp's "readymades" revealed the true nature of this culture to itself.[5] It is the story of a continuing strategy of modernism to "provoke, disappoint, and in the end displace the aesthetic expectations which, in this or that moment, constitute pictorial taste. In any case, the stakes for modernism has not been either [artistic] taste or a theory [of art], it has been the name. The conflicts between avant-garde and tradition . . . have revolved about the name one gives to 'painting.'"[6]

The thesis Thierry de Duve is advancing is that Duchamp's "readymades," as exemplified in *Fountain,* are simply the culmination of a long history in the art world of what he calls "pictorial nominalism" and I call "aesthetic nominalism." Nominalism, however, is a word many readers might not be familiar with. "Pictorial nominalism" or "aesthetic nominalism" is, in my mind, the analogue of epistemological nominalism. Epistemological nominalism refers to a great philosophical debate that began in the Middle Ages and continues to this day. The issue can be put succintly in a question: What's in a name?

It is the debate whether names refer to some reality or are simply made up by us as a mental sign. The issue is important. It is about beliefs on the nature of reality. Is reality interconnected? Is an apple from this tree connected in a real way to an apple from some other tree? If so, then the name apple truly refers to a reality that connects these two particular apples.[7] On the other hand, if one believes that reality is not interconnected, that there exists only concrete individual objects in the universe, then "apple" amounts to a mere name made up to help us talk about particular apples. The name "apple" has no other reality but in our mind. As you can see, epistemological nominalism tends to make an extremely sharp distinction between the world outside the mind, and the mind itself. The world cannot be known in any direct way. All we have is language and mental constructs to refer to the world. What kind of art would such a view envision? Such art would be found less in the physical, material work of art than in the mind of the artist himself.

Consider, for example, Duchamp's justification of his "readymade" as a work of art. "Whether Mr. Mutt with his own hands made the fountain or not has no importance. He CHOSE it. He took an ordinary article of life, placed it so that its useful significance disappeared under a new title and point of view—[he] created a new thought for that object."[8] Duchamp is telling us that for him the ultimate end of art is a "thought." This belief is consistent with the nominalism debated in the Middle Ages. It is also consistent with the contemporary view that the individual has almost absolute autonomy in his actions and her thoughts.

Epistemological nominalism, because of its sharp distinctions between the mind and reality, leads to great number of dichotomies: mind and matter, individual and community, nature and culture, body and soul, and so on. These dichotomies also happen to describe a legacy of thought we have inherited and in which we now find ourselves devilishly entangled. Epistemological nominalism also has social consequences. The individual is prized above and over the community. Even worse, it is felt that our actions have few if any consequences beyond one's own individual little world. This last consequence plays out in the world of art as Duchamp's indifference to the work of art. In the "readymades" of Duchamp, nominalism emerges as proposing the ultimate dichotomy between the artist and his art.

Duchamp's "readymades" represent all sorts of artistic dualisms: the artist versus his art, the avant-garde versus traditional style, the museum versus the home, art versus craft, genius versus non-aesthete, and, unfortunately, religion versus art. Nominalism, as it has affected art, has made the artist an individual unto him and herself. It has encouraged the artist to continually produce works of novelty at the expense of style. It has encouraged the commodification of art such that art can be invested in at auctions that act as some sort of artistic stock exchange. It has encouraged the alienation of works of art from the everyday life of ordinary people. It has encouraged a passive aesthetics where art is simply hung up on the wall to be viewed. It has encouraged art to become elitist only to be enjoyed by those who share in a very private knowledge of art. Indeed, art has encouraged a very specialized knowledge of itself inaccessible to ordinary people.

Picasso put it well when he spoke of the current dilemma the artist faces: "Beginning with van Gogh, however great we may be, we are all, in a measure, autodidacts—you might almost say, primitive painters no longer live within a tradition and so each one of us must re-create an entire language from A to Z. No criterion can be applied to him a priori, since we don't believe in rigid standards any longer. In a certain sense, that's a liberation; but at the same time, it's an enormous limitation, because when the individuality of the artist begins to express itself, what the artist gains in liberty he loses in the way of order. And when you're no longer able to attach yourself to an order, basically, that's very bad."[9]

Though this statement was made in 1902, it describes the nominalism that celebrates the individuality of the artist. As Ernst Gombrich, the great art critic, said of this statement by Picasso: "There is no such thing as 'art,' there are only individual artists."[10] Such absolute individualism is a direct consequence of nominalism and comes at the expense of those relationships (i.e., universals) that speak of a wider world, a world beyond individualism, a world, that is, of community and tradition.

Nominalism has indeed affected the art world. One can tell "aesthetic nominalism" at work by its symptoms:[11]

(1) The rupture of the bond between the aesthetics of a work of art and artistic innovation. The beauty of a work of art has much to do with the creativity of the artist. Unfortunately, the artistic trend Duchamp represents is one in which artistic innovation feeds on the artist's freedom by requiring more and more innovation. The artist having created a novel piece of art must now betray his discovery and produce something completely different. It is as if the need for artistic innovation asks of the artist a creative power approaching the *ex nihilo* creative power once attributed only to God. It also destroys the development and cultivation of style and encourages contentious splintering among artists.

(2) The loss of general rules for artistic production. There is no real attempt to discover or describe norms that might distinguish a good work of art from a "bad" work of art. Such art requires the observer to try to figure out what the artist is up to rather than try to understand the work of art itself. Such art almost cries out to its audience to give it a "name" instead of calling forth the recognition of artistic skill. As such, it encourages the formation of elite groups, or, if I may borrow the language of religion, art "gnostics," who have special knowledge that "unlock" the puzzle of the artwork that is before them.[12]

(3) The loss of conviction in the reality of universals including that special universal, the transcendental of beauty. Such loss tends to divide the art community. The art world begins to be plagued by contentious splintering as one avant-garde group "rebels" against the efforts and point of view of another. Worse yet, lack of a belief in the reality of universals encourages a view of art that distances it from reality. Art, in this view, has more to do with ideas than with reality. As such, art has very little to say to the non-art world. Art discloses no truths about the universe, society, or even the human spirit. It alienates art from every other dimension of human life and creates an almost esoteric group of individuals. It allows art to be subject to Plato's sharp attack that art is essentially removed from reality therefore it is to be shunned.

(4) The sole purpose seen for art is that of exhibition and there is no orientation for human ends. In the church, anyway, artworks fulfill many other purposes. It serves the needs of the community for instruction, assembling, and prayer. In other words, art is oriented to human ends as well as being exhibited. In the modern art world, the many purposes of art seem to be terribly restricted to that of exhibition in a museum or gallery or the private home of a very wealthy collector. Danto himself raises this issue. There exists, he says, "a deep question of whether exhibition or display is appropriate to [works of art]."[13] Indeed, aesthetic nominalism encourages works of art to be exhibition objects rather than a "response to human ends."[14] Exhibition creates an aesthetic distance or as Berstein put, "an aesthetic alienation." Aesthetic nominalism, in other words, takes away the dignity of works of art by reducing them to objects for exhibition rather than works related to human ends.

(5) A loss of reverence for the relations that make up the lives of everyday individuals. Aesthetic nominalism encourages artists to become abstracted

from the concerns and issues of society and of everyday life. More distressing to the theologian, aesthetic nominalism discourages the seeking of religious insight into the spiritual struggles in most people's lives. Such art becomes irrelevant to the human condition and one can ask about the nature of its humanism. Perhaps, worse, such art fails to engage in any profound way the very nature of human spirituality as it manifests itself in artistic creativity. As such, art's very creativity runs the danger of becoming idiosyncratic or sterile.

These, then, are the symptoms of aesthetic nominalism. They describe a sickness of the human spirit that needs urgent attention. The treatment for this sickness is a more profound engagement with the nature of the human spirit. What is needed is the re-articulation of a new humanism. I believe a major contribution to this new humanism can be found in the theological dimension of art.

The Theological Dimension of Art

Any attempt to describe the theological dimension of art must overcome a variety of obstacles that have to do with distinctions and definitions. How does the theological dimension of art, for example, differ from the religious dimension? Or the spiritual dimension? What role does experience play in the theological dimension of art? Indeed, what role does experience play in art? It is here where the American philosophical tradition via Peirce, Royce, and Dewey can be very helpful. First, however, let me tackle a couple of fine distinctions and take a stab at one important definition.

One ought to distinguish between the religious and the spiritual. Though often seen as synonymous, they are usually not. Religious art, by its very nature, is iconic. It is specific to its religious subject. Thus, religious art plays with images specific to a religion. Whether it is a sculpture of the Buddha or a painting of the Madonna, religious art aims at the belief system of its beholder. Its aim, however, is not to deepen the faith of the beholder but, rather, to activate it. As such, the quality of the art itself is not as important, its value lies in its ability to activate the mind and heart to the tenets of a faith. It leads the beholder to prayer. A true example of this kind of art is the Russian Orthodox *ikon*.[15]

The spiritual, on the other hand, may not be an image specific to a religion. It does, however, have the power to move the heart. And it does so in a way that is nonconceptual. As Sister Wendy Beckett puts it "[art] effects what it signifies, (to use an old catechism definition of a sacrament), but the mind may be aware only of the impact of some mysterious truth. This is the essence of spiritual art. We are taken into a realm that is potentially open to us, *we are made more what we are meant to be*."[16] These distinctions are not absolute. There are works of art that are both religious and spiritual such as Caravaggio's *The Incredulity of St. Thomas*. Sister Wendy, however, is silent about the theological dimension of art.

The silence judges the present status of theological investigation. Theology has distanced itself from the spiritual and, even, the religious. It has either become a means to reconcile doctrinal conflicts (which is a legitimate vocation of theology) or a means to become a prophetic voice for those who have few other advocates in society (again, another legitimate use of theology). While either of these elements in theology are legitimate, they deteriorate into a narrow parochialism or strident moralism without the spiritual and religious dimension. Von Balthasar addressed this theological malaise in a famous article on "Theology and Sanctity."[17]

Theology not only ought to address the mind or the thirst for justice but also the heart of devotion and transformation. Theology and sanctity are one piece. Together, they encompass the spiritual and religious dimensions of which Sister Wendy Beckett so eloquently speaks and add their own unique dimension. The theological dimension of art does not simply concern the spiritual or religious dimension in a work of art but also its insights into the transformation of the human creature and the power of such art to evoke loyalty and devotion to one another and to the divine. The theological dimension of a work of art concerns religious insight in the experience of art.

Perhaps one of the greatest insights into the nature of art is by the great American philosopher, John Dewey. He saw "art as experience." Indeed, this is the title of his famous book. Dewey's great gift to us is his insight into the nature of experience. Experience is, perhaps, the most misunderstood and most elusive of terms. Nonetheless, it is a term that has real meaning. Experience, for Dewey, cannot be synonymous with consciousness or with the mind. Experience has to do with a vast complex of abilities and acts that connect an organism intelligently to its world. Thus, experience can stem from subconscious drives, prereflective habits, or acts of cold, calculated reason.[18]

Experience, according to Dewey, is intrinsically temporal. Ideas do not simply come out of thin air. They are embedded in a set of connected relationships which unfold with a sense of "whence" and "whither." The temporal element in experience is best seen in aesthetic experience. The classical understanding of aesthetic experience was as the copy of an eternal form. Dewey sees aesthetic experience as the development of a process: "Instead of being a glimpse of a timeless reality, aesthetic experience is a rhythmic development arising from the interaction of the organism and the object leading toward a sense of purpose, wholeness, and integration, closing in a pervasive sense of meaning."[19]

This understanding of experience and especially, aesthetic experience, has certain philosophical consequences. First, aesthetic experience leads somewhere. It is full of meaning and purpose. Thus, Art, for Dewey, has as its important mission making life meaningful. Second, aesthetic experience is embodied. Experience is not some mental process. It is neither propositional nor cognitive. In other words, experience is not about making judgments. Finally, by locating aesthetic experience in common experience, Dewey blurs the line between "fine arts" and ordinary life. It is not that Dewey does not admit the possibility of a "fine arts" but that such art would not exist if it were not for an underlying common experience of life. As Dewey put it: "Mountain peaks [of experience] do not float unsupported; they do not even rest upon the earth; they are the earthy in one of its manifest operations."[20] The significance of Dewey's approach is that Art is once again placed within the ordinary rhythms of life. Art's home is not simply the museum hall but also the hall of our own home.

Dewey's reflections on experience and art as experience are a balm to a world that pits the work of art against the artist, the museum against the home, refined sensibility against vital sensibility, indeed, the artistic against the religious, the spiritual, and the theological. For in Dewey's understanding of Art and experience lies the foundation for articulating a theological dimension of art. Dewey's understanding of Art as experience lends itself to the philosophical notion of religious insight.

Religious insight is a special term in the American philosophical tradition. It is a term developed in opposition to the deficiencies noted in the description of a religious experience. William James described religious experience as a consequence of psychological processes in his famous book, *The Variety of Religious Experiences*.[21] Josiah Royce saw an immediate problem with this understanding of religious experience. It made religious experience a largely private and individual affair. The communal dimension of religious experience is almost impossible with

James' psychological approach. Thus, Royce proposed as alternative to *a variety of religious experiences,* a look at the *sources of religious insight.*[22]

By insight Royce meant a special kind of knowledge. As he put it: "Insight is knowledge that makes us aware of the unity of many facts in one whole, and that at the same time brings us into intimate personal contact with these facts and with the whole wherein they are united. The three marks of insight are breadth of range, coherence and unity of view, and closeness of personal touch."[23] What this means is that insight is knowledge that not only has breadth and coherence but is also close and personal. Note how different insight, as Royce describes it, is from the detached knowledge attributed to mathematics and science. Insight is knowledge whose home is experience yet needs more than experience. Insight connects experience with a larger world. As such, insight contains some of the elements of an innocence. To be connected to a larger world involves some measure of innocence. The cynic will find it hard to reach any sort of insight.

Yet this is not yet religious insight. For Royce, religion essentially deals with redemption, that is in "freeing mankind from some vast and universal burden, of imperfection, of unworthiness, or of sin."[24] Religious insight, then, is defined by its object. Religious insight is, as he puts it, "insight into need and into the way of salvation."[25] Religious insight, Royce felt, might be a way for the diversity of religions to find a common element. Rather than have religions look at the particularity of religious experience, let them look at the sources of their religious insight. Perhaps, then, religions may find their unity, for all of them will, in one way or another, drink from these same sources.

What are these sources? Royce mentions individual and social experience, the office of the reason, the world and the will, loyalty, and, what he called, the religious mission of sorrow. There is one source Royce felt he should add, but did not have the courage to do so: the beautiful. The beautiful, for Royce, was, perhaps, the most profound source of religious insight. He felt, however, that the topic was greater than his understanding of it, therefore he declined to give an account of it as a source.[26] Nonetheless, the beautiful is found all over his writings. It is here that I take a certain liberty with Royce's thought.

I find Royce's religious insight a marvelous way to describe theology. Theology, I believe, is faith seeking understanding. Theology, however, is also bringing such understanding to the whirlwind that is the world of believers and unbelievers, Christian and non-Christian, just and the unjust. To that whirlwind, theology does have something to offer: Royce's religious insight, insight into the need and way of salvation. As such, theology can be a guide to those who are seeking more than religious experience or spiritual power. Theology can offer religious insight into the human condition.

Theology as religious insight reveals another dimension. Such theology involves a marvelous innocence. Not despairing or cynical but ever-hoping, and believing in all things, religious insight enters into the vocation of theology as a marvelous innocence that engages the world's imagination. The need for salvation requires, after all, a certain humility that is tantamount to an achieved innocence. Innocence is the virtue for those who see their need of salvation. Art is, in a deep sense, the perfect medium for this innocence. In art, theology finds one of its most important missions, an indispensable element of its vocation. By this I mean theology's vocation to bring insight of the need and way of salvation in its reflections on the social and cultural environment it finds itself in.

In the arts, this element of theology's vocation finds its most powerful medium. Though art has been used in the Church as a way to evoke the presence of the divine, as a spiritual way to communion with God, and in the service of the Church's message and doctrine, art, in our day, can become a source of religious insight for theology. Theology can find in art profound spiritual struggles that speak to the possibility of human self-transcendence. Theology can use its experience and discipline to detect traces of a spiritual struggle that might go undetected otherwise. At the same time, theology can learn from what it discovers. Art has much to teach theology about the struggle of the spirit in the world. As such, theology uncovers a dimension of art that might go unnoticed while, at the same time, opening up theology to new forms of insight. It is in this mutual insight that the theological dimension of art is to be found.

The theological dimension of art, let me propose, is the religious insight into the need and way of salvation that has as its source the beautiful in the form of a work of art. Let us see how this proposal works in the case of Duchamp's *Fountain*.

Finding the Theological Dimension in Duchamp's Fountain

Paul Tillich, the great Lutheran theologian, once wrote of art: "every style points to a self-interpretation of man, thus answering the question of the meaning of life. Whatever the subject-matter which an artist chooses . . . he cannot help but betray by his style his own ultimate concern as well as that of his group, and his period."[27] Tillich's great insight into the theological dimension of art is that a work of art reveals not simply the concerns of the individual artist but also of the entire community that directly (or indirectly) supports the artist.[28] A work of art does not stand simply as a unique expression of an individual artist but also expresses the deepest concerns of the artist's community.

If this is so, then Marcel Duchamp's *Fountain* presents the theologian a disturbing puzzle. What deep social and religious concerns does *Fountain* express? What possible "ultimate concern" could an ordinary urinal picked up at a common hardware store and simply signed by the artist express? Instead, *Fountain* plays havoc with any high-minded theory of art. Duchamp appears to mock the concerns of the very community that brands his off-the-hardware-shelf urinal a "work of art." Indeed, Duchamp's *Fountain* mocks art itself.

In 1964, for example, the well-known philosopher Arthur Danto walked into a curious exhibition that took place at the avant-garde Stable Gallery. Stacks of Brillo boxes were piled all over the place. The place looked less like a gallery than a warehouse for surplus scouring pads. The Stable Gallery was exhibiting the latest work of the artist Andy Warhol. The exhibition shocked Danto. He could see no real difference between these Brillo pads as everyday objects and their new status as art objects.

Danto's first reaction to this "work of art" was, in his own words, a profound "aesthetic repugnance." As he began to reflect further, however, he began to see a sophisticated audience, an audience that knew its art history, actually enjoying the exhibition. Danto's "aesthetic repugnance" now became overwhelmed by "philosophical intoxication." The response of the sophisticated audience to Warhol's Brillo cartons suggested to Danto that the "end of art" had arrived. "It has not *stopped* but ended, in the sense that it has passed over into a kind of consciousness of itself and become, again in a way, its own philosophy: a state of affairs predicted in Hegel's philosophy of history."[29]

Danto is not the only one who has noticed that something has ended (even if not "stopped") in art. J. M. Bernstein, for example, laments the "Fate of Art" has fallen into an insidious state of "aesthetic alienation."[30] Jean-Marie Schaeffer distresses over the "abstruse, hollow gibberish" found in "French art journals" indicating the "minimalist dead end at which several sectors of the visual arts have arrived."[31] George Pattison observes that "the path of modern art, pursued to the bitter end, led to no promised land; there was no rainbow bridge leading from earth to the land of everlasting beauty; there was only the bleak wasteland of aesthetic nihilism."[32]

Peter Fuller believes that the "aesthetic dimension" of art has been betrayed in "Late Modernism" creating a condition of "General Anesthesia."[33] Thierry de Duve calls the situation after Duchamp an era of "anartiste" or, again, "Pictorial Nominalism."[34] "Aesthetic alienation," "aesthetic nihilism," "minimalist dead end," "Anaesthesia," "Pictorial Nominalism" and the "end of art" could have been opinions of Duchamp's "Fountain." Instead they describe a general sense of frustration with the visual arts of today. They also describe a set of "wounds." These "wounds" are not only philosophical but also spiritual, religious, and social. Duchamp's *Fountain* could as easily be seen as the woundedness of Modernity. As such, these "wounds" are also symptoms of an "aesthetic nominalism."

Given such a diagnosis, is it possible for Duchamp's *Fountain* to possess a theological dimension? I believe so if we understand that dimension as described above, as a religious insight into the need and way of salvation which has the beautiful in the form of a work of art as its source. Duchamp's *Fountain* taxes the limits of such a proposal. It is for this reason that *Fountain* is ideal to raise the question of a theological dimension in art. The first clue that *Fountain* contains a theological dimension comes from Arthur Danto.

Danto became aware of an ancient philosophical issue embedded in Duchamp's *Fountain*. What is the status of a work of art to reality? Or, as Heidegger might have put it, what is the relationship of a work of art to a "mere, real thing"? Danto noticed that Duchamp's "readymades" raise this ancient issue in a strikingly modern way. What makes Duchamp's urinal different from an ordinary urinal? Duchamp's urinal, after all, is not a copy of an original. It is the original. On the other hand, Duchamp's *Fountain* is one of many identical copies mass produced. Indeed, modern technology raises a certain conundrum about the relationship of a work of art to its subject. In the final analysis, however, Duchamp's *Fountain* amounts to an attack on art as something thrice removed from reality. Like Plato, Duchamp's urinal as work of art makes the point that only the mind knows the true nature of a thing. We only know the urinal is a work of art because it exists as such in Duchamp's creative mind.

What Danto didn't discern was the profound theological dimension behind the issue. Duchamp's *Fountain* offers true religious insight into the human condition. The question as to the relationship of a work of art to a "mere, real thing" is, after all, also a question that can be asked of a sacrament. What is the relationship of consecrated bread to ordinary bread? Consecrated wine to ordinary wine? Baptismal water to ordinary water? Anointing oil to ordinary oil? When does the stuff of our ordinary lives become something sacred? Somewhere in the answer to that question, I believe, we will also find the theological dimension that Duchamp's *Fountain* dares us to address.

What, then, makes a piece of ordinary bread a sacred reality? One need not get into esoteric sacramental theology for this exploration to take place. Certainly one of the crucial elements of a sacrament is that it is a sign but it is a sign that addresses the participant in his and her whole being. A sacrament as sacred sign does not solely address our minds, though it does this as well. Neither does a sacrament as sacred sign simply appeal to our emotions though it also does this. A sacrament as sacred sign does not even solely address our spiritual side. A sacrament addresses the whole person, body and soul. A sacrament, in other words, calls for insight. A holistic but close and personal knowledge about our human condition.

Another crucial element of a sacrament is a community that interprets the sacrament for the present by looking to its past heritage and contrasting it to its future promise. Thus, an ordinary piece of bread begins to take a very special meaning when we speak the words "Christ has died, Christ is risen, Christ will come again." A sacrament, in other words, has all the marks of what Dewey called the temporal dimension of experience. As such, the temporal dimension of sacraments is an experience. Moreover, it is an aesthetic experience in the sense Dewey meant, for in the temporal dimension of a sacrament, one experiences less a "glimpse of a timeless reality," than the transformation of the "rhythmic development" arising from sorrows and vagaries of life into "a sense of purpose, wholeness, and integration, closing in a pervasive sense of meaning."[35]

Even more, a sacrament is an experience that is very personal even as it is only possible in community. For it is the past, present, and future of a community that becomes part of the rhythm and life of the particular individual. The past, present, and future of the community now become inextricable with the past, present, and future of the particular individual. More crucial to the nature of a sacrament is the sense that it allows us to participate in a reality that is not truly ours. In other words, in sacraments, one can experience a kind of human transcendence that is also at the same time a kind of divine immanence. A sacrament allows us to experience a transcendent presence that is felt to be redemptive. Indeed, the redemptive dimension of a sacrament is the most crucial of all.

A sacrament addresses, after all, the wounded, who, by definition, are those who know the need of salvation. A sacrament dresses the wounds of our suffering and heals us by offering insight into the way of salvation. A sacrament, then, is an aesthetic experience that offers not only insight but religious insight into the need and way of salvation. As such, a sacrament's religious insight engenders a certain attitude on the participant. Through the woundedness of our life, sacramental insight breaks out in a felt experience of healing and transformation into a special type of awareness on the part of the participant. This awareness is very difficult to describe. It is experienced as a type of "seeing," a kind of openness to all sorts of undreamed of possibilities. As such, the sacraments evoke a marvelous innocence, an openness to a larger world than our own that emerges not in spite of our wounds but because of them. This sort of insight gained from the wounds and sorrows in our life and touched by the sacramental grace of a divine love describes a wondrous innocence; indeed, sacraments describe *a wounded innocence.*

The religious insight sacraments offer addresses the theological dimension of Duchamp's *Fountain. Fountain* exposes the human condition of Modernity. Through the philosophical, religious, spiritual, artistic, and social questions it raises, *Fountain* reveals the woundedness of the Modern condition. As such, Duchamp's *Fountain* makes clear the need of salvation and engenders a hunger for insight into the way of salvation. The theological dimension of Duchamp's *Fountain* is the need of religious insight in art today. A look at the religious insight intrinsic to sacraments helped unravel this hidden dimension. Sacraments, ironically, become a sacrament to the philosophical, religious, spiritual, artistic, and social wounds exposed by Duchamp's *Fountain.* The religious insight afforded by sacraments reveals as well the nature of art's religious insight. The need and way of salvation involves a marvelous innocence achieved only in our woundedness. The theological dimension of art is, indeed, *a wounded innocence.*

1. William Camfield, "Marcel Duchamp's Fountain: Aesthetic Object, Icon, or Anti-Art?" in *The Definitively Unfinished Marcel Duchamp,* edited by Thierry de Duve (Halifax, N.S./Cambridge, Mass.: Nova Scotia College of Art and Design/MIT Press, 1991) 137.

2. Ibid., 133.

3. Calvin Tomkins and Time-Life Books, *The World of Marcel Duchamp, 1887–1968,* edited by Time-Life Books (Alexandria, Va./Morristown, N.J.: Time-Life Books school and library distribution by Silver Burdett Co., 1977) 16.

4. Translation mine. I am translating "peinture" (lit. "painting") as "art" throughout because I believe that is the intention of the author Thierry de Duve, *Nominalisme Pictural Marcel Duchamp, la Peinture et la Modernité,* Collection "Critique" (Paris: Editions de Minuit, 1984) 32.

5. Duve, op. cit., 33.

6. Translation mine; Duve, op. cit., 131.

7. The interested reader is directed to the following sources: Jan Aertsen, *Medieval Philosophy and the Transcendentals the Case of Thomas Aquinas,* Studien und Texte Zur Geistesgeschichte Des Mittelalters (Leiden/New York: E. J. Brill, 1996); Johannes Baptist Lotz, "Transcendentals," in *Sacramentum Mundi,* vol. 6, edited by Karl Rahner (New York: Herder and Herder, 1970), 285–87; Heiko Augustinus Oberman, *The Harvest of Medieval Theology: Gabriel Biel and Late Medieval Nominalism,* rev. ed. (Grand Rapids, Mich.: William B. Eerdmans, 1967); Allan Bernard Wolter, *The Transcendentals and Their Function in the Metaphysics of Duns Scotus* (Washington, D. C.: The Catholic University of America Press, 1946).

8. Quoted in Tomkins and Time-Life Books, op. cit., 39.

9. Picasso to Françoise Gilot as quoted in Arthur Coleman Danto, *Beyond the Brillo Box: The Visual Arts in Post-Historical Perspective* (Berkeley: University of California Press, 1998) 128–29.

10. Quoted in Danto, *Beyond the Brillo Box: The Visual Arts in Post-Historical Perspective,* 129.

11. The following "symptoms" are my appropriation of the work done by Charles Peirce on nominalism as well as the work of Duve, especially Duve, op. cit., 132–34.

12. I do not wish to be misunderstood here, however. General rules for artistic production are not a limitation of artistic freedom. They are a belief, however, that a community of observers can recognize the worth of a work of art and not depend on the "name" of the style given to an art work.

13 Danto, *Beyond the Brillo Box: The Visual Arts in Post-Historical Perspective,* 112.

14. Ibid., 129.

15. Much of the above and what follows comes from the fine exposition found in Wendy Beckett, *Art and the Sacred: The Mystical Now* (New York: Universe, 1993) 5–26.

16. Emphasis mine; Beckett, op. cit., 7.

17. Hans Urs von Balthasar, "Theology and Sanctity," in *The Word Made Flesh,* vol. 1, Explorations in Theology (San Francisco: Ignatius Press, 1989) 181–209.

18. Thomas M. Alexander and John Dewey, "John Dewey's Theory of Art, Experience, and Nature the Horizons of Feeling," in *Classical American Pragmatism: Its Contemporary Validity,* SUNY Series in Philosophy (Albany, N.Y.: State University of New York Press, 1987) 164.

19. Ibid., 165.

20. John Dewey, *Art as Experience,* reprint, 1934, Perigee Books (New York: The Berkley Publishing Group, 1980) 3.

21. William James, *The Varieties of Religious Experience: A Study in Human Nature* (New York: Longmans, Green, 1902).

22. *The Sources of Religious Insight* became Royce's famous critique of James' psychological approach to religious experience. Experience is more than a psychological event, it engages the intellect as well as the senses in the context of a communal process of interpreting life and its reality. Thus, religious experience is best seen as religious insight. Josiah Royce, *The Sources of Religious Insight Lectures* (New York: Scribner, 1912).

23. Royce, op. cit., 5–6.

24. Ibid., 8.

25. Ibid., 17.

26. In a letter to Richard Cabot dated June 25, 1912, Royce wrote, "Yes, beauty is a 'source' that my list ought to have contained. . . . My omission of that source is a defect, and needs a simple confession as such, although I believe that I have never heretofore told you what I suppose to be the nature and source of this defect in my view of such things. Personally, I have *some* access to beauty especially in *two* realms, viz.; music, and nature-beauty; together with a fairly warm, but, as you know, limited access to poetry. As to music and nature-beauty, I am, and must remain, naïve, ignorant—at best childlike. My own childhood was passed in a mining town, and later in S[an] F[rancisco]. I never saw any beautiful object that man had made until I was twenty years, I left California for Germany. . . . Of beauty, therefore, I must not prophesy. The less I say about beauty, the more sincere will be, and sound, the little that I have any right on occasion to stammer. . . . So here is the defect. It is subjective and insignificant. What beauty I *have* known has meant to me some things that I long to say, if I might, and that have brightened the world for me with a light that I deeply wish to be able to characterize. But it all remains for me, in *this* life, either unutterable, or tragic, or sacred. . . . Read me then, always subject to this defect, which you, or anybody, must condemn, without my being able to defend myself." Josiah Royce and John Clendenning, *The Letters of Josiah Royce,* edited by John Clendenning (Chicago: University of Chicago Press, 1970) 577–8.

27. Paul Tillich, Jane Dillenberger, and John Dillenberger, *On Art and Architecture,* edited by Jane Dillenberger, translated by Jane Dillenberger (New York: Crossroad, 1987) 121.

28. The community of the artist does not only include those who directly support the artist by participating in gallery exhibitions of his or her work but also the community that creates the wider social structures in which the artist must live and create his or her art.

29. Arthur Coleman Danto, *The Transfiguration of the Commonplace: A Philosophy of Art* (Cambridge, Mass.: Harvard University Press, 1981) vii.

30. J. M. Bernstein, *The Fate of Art: Aesthetic Alienation from Kant to Derrida and Adorno,* Literature and Philosophy (University Park, Pa.: Pennsylvania State University Press, 1992).

31. Jean-Marie Schaeffer, *Art of the Modern Age: Philosophy of Art from Kant to Heidegger,* New French Thought (Princeton, N.J.: Princeton University Press, 2000) 4–5.

32. George Pattison, *Art, Modernity, and Faith: Restoring the Image* (London: SCM Press, 1998) 2.

33. Peter Fuller and Power Institute of Fine Arts, *Aesthetics After Modernism* (London, England/New York: Writers and Readers Distributed in the U.S.A. by Norton, 1983) 12.

34. Duve, op. cit.

35. Dewey, op. cit.

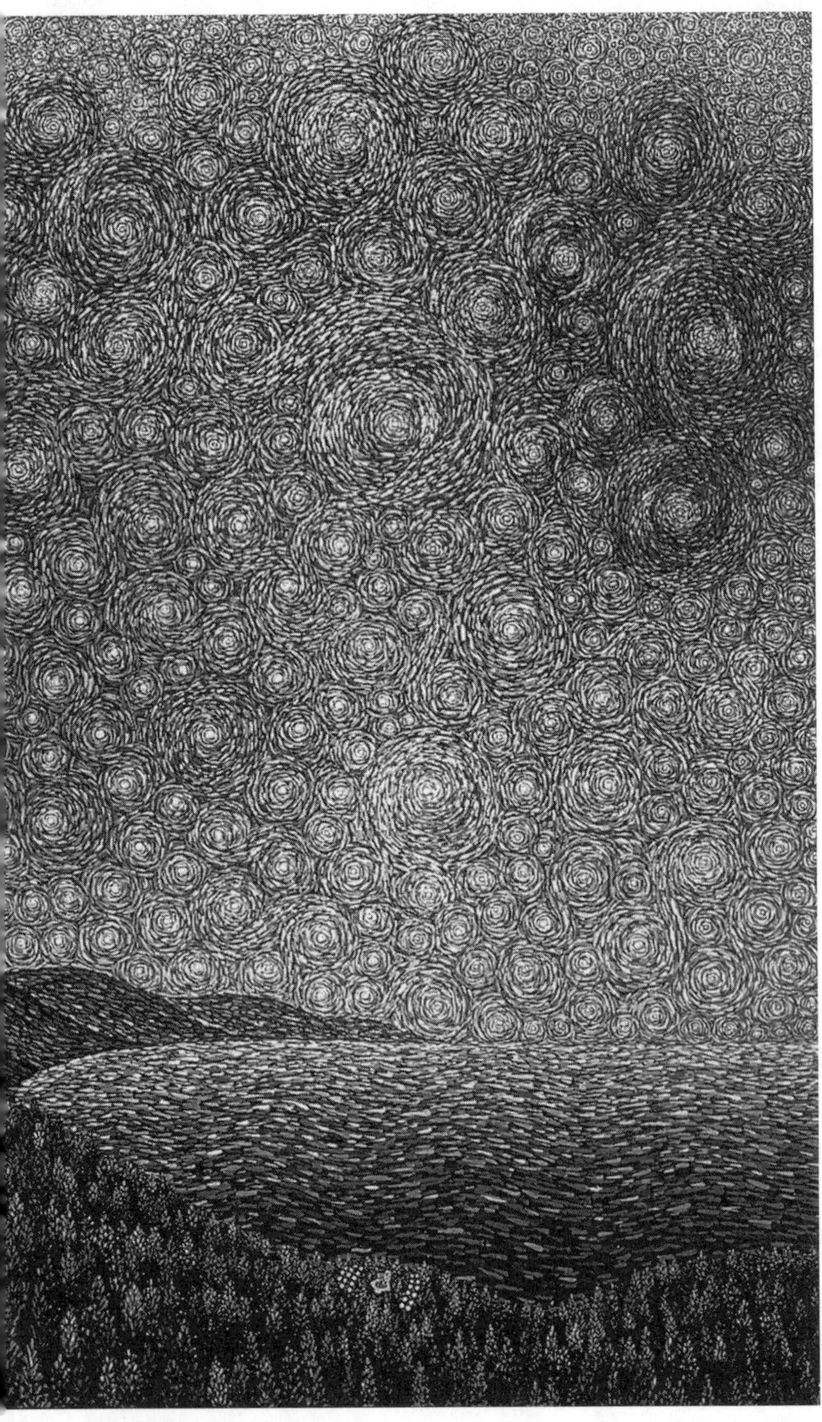

"Christmas Sky at the Hermitage"

CHAPTER THREE

Human Freedom and Artistic Creativity

THE LITTLE RULE OF MASTER ROMUALD

SIT IN YOUR CELL AS IN PARADISE. PUT THE WHOLE WORLD BEHIND YOU AND FORGET IT. WATCH YOUR THOUGHTS LIKE A GOOD FISHERMAN WATCHING FOR FISH.

THE PATH YOU MUST FOLLOW IS IN THE PSALMS—NEVER LEAVE IT.

IF YOU HAVE JUST COME TO THE MONASTERY, AND IN SPITE OF YOUR GOOD WILL YOU CANNOT ACCOMPLISH WHAT YOU WANT, THEN TAKE EVERY OPPORTUNITY YOU CAN TO SING THE PSALMS IN YOUR HEART AND TO UNDERSTAND THEM WITH YOUR MIND. AND IF YOUR MIND WANDERS AS YOU READ, DO NOT GIVE UP; HURRY BACK AND APPLY YOUR MIND TO THE WORDS ONCE MORE.

REALIZE ABOVE ALL THAT YOU ARE IN GOD'S PRESENCE, AND STAND THERE WITH THE ATTITUDE OF ONE WHO STANDS BEFORE THE EMPEROR.

EMPTY YOURSELF COMPLETELY AND SIT WAITING, CONTENT WITH THE GRACE OF GOD, LIKE THE CHICK WHO TASTES NOTHING AND EATS NOTHING BUT WHAT HIS MOTHER BRINGS HIM.[1]

A Powerful Freedom

In the last chapter, I sketched what the theological dimension of a work of art might look like. The theological dimension of a work of art, I proposed, encompasses both the religious and the spiritual dimensions by giving religious insight into the need and way of salvation. As such, a work of art has spiritual kinship to a sacrament. I said little, however, about the spiritual nature of the experience of a work of art. Modern aesthetics approaches such experience as either the interior subjectivity of a beholder or the inventive expressiveness of the artist. As such, the artistic experience, in modern terms, has an intrinsic dualism. Either one can speak of the experience of the beholder or the experience of the artistic process. There is little room to speak of both as one integrated experience. That is unless you are a Camaldolese monk.

Arthur Poulin is a hermit. Rather, he is part of a community of monks that have a hermit tradition, the Camaldolese. As such, Fr. Poulin is best described as a hermit-monk. The reader might find it strange, however, to see a work of art by a hermit-monk to extol the virtues of the communal dimension in art. Aren't hermits rugged individuals who go off by themselves in order to avoid community? The answer to this last question is "No." At least, the answer is "No" for Camaldolese hermit-monks. For Arthur Poulin is a member of the Camaldolese Order that has its roots in the monastic reforms initiated by St. Romuald in the eleventh century.

These monastic reforms included the recognition that the common life of a monk and the solitary life of the hermit need and sustain each other. As such, the Camaldolese hermit-monk gives an alternative vision of how one can be a "rugged" individual without forsaking community. And it is this twin dimension of individual and community that has proved fertile for Arthur Poulin's artistic creativity. This chapter explores Arthur's artistic method in the context of the Camaldolese community that has proved fertile ground for his aesthetic visions. As such, an insight into the theological dimension of art will become evident. The theological dimension of art involves the commingling of two freedoms which finds analogy in the mingling of the freedom of the individual and the demands of a community.

St. Romuald's little rule, however, allows us a view of the spiritual that will, I believe, give us another religious insight into the nature of the artistic experience. To see this, one must take a deeper look at the nature of artistic freedom and its spiritual dimension. Aesthetic nominalism, as the last chapter demonstrated, demands of the artist a certain kind of creative freedom that approaches the absolute creative freedom attributed to God. The demands of such absolute freedom, moreover, tends to alienate the artist from the wider community, and, even worse, from art itself. It is well, then, to contrast this absolute creative freedom to the freedom of the hermit as suggested in St. Romuald's little rule.

Being a hermit, after all, speaks of a powerful freedom. The Camaldolese hermit seeks freedom from illusions, his own as well as those from the world outside his cell. This freedom, however, is not freedom from the world, that is a *fuga mundi*. It is a more complex liberty. At stake in the little rule of St. Romuald is the possibility of self-transcendence. Self-transcendence, however, is not the result of some absolute exercise of human freedom. Self-transcendence is sought as a gift, a meal brought to the chick by its mother. Indeed, self-transcendence is sought in the meeting of two freedoms, the hermit's human freedom and God's Divine Freedom. The powerful freedom of the hermit is found in his willingness to be shaped and formed by the gracious art of Divine Freedom.

As such, St. Romuald's little rule reveals a profound insight into the spiritual nature of artistic freedom. Human freedom emerges from and finds its fulfillment in Divine Freedom. This insight is not unique to St. Romuald. An ancient analogy exists between God as Creator and an artist's creativity that serves as a model for the relationship between human and Divine freedom.[2] Indeed, John Paul II in his *Letter to Artists* calls artists the "image of God the Creator."[3] This analogy notes the difference between Creator God and creative artist. God the Creator alone has absolute freedom in creating. God the Creator "bestows being itself" while the creative artist "uses something that already exists, to which he gives form and meaning."[4]

An artist's work ultimately becomes a sign of this relationship between God's creative freedom and the artist's human freedom. Just as the hermit struggles with his own freedom in order to receive a greater one, the artist also struggles with his or her own freedom in the presence of an awesome and absolute Divine Freedom. As such, the work of art reveals much about the artist's struggle with his or her own freedom. This struggle is given vision in the artist's personal style. It is for this reason that even in the 30,000-year-old paintings at Lascaux, one can sense the struggles and hopes of souls unknown to us but now expressed in the creative way those ancient artists depicted the animals that were so much a part of their way of life.

Aesthetic nominalism, on the other hand, so emphasizes the freedom of the artist to create that the ultimate expression of the artist's work is freedom itself rather than an actual work. Indeed, so emphasizing the freedom of the artist over the constraints inherent in a concrete work of art destroys the very nature of artistic creativity. And with the demise of creativity, so goes the spiritual element in a work of art. For creativity involves both struggle and vision. The artist not only struggles creatively with the constraints of the medium of his and her art in order to give expression to the vision. The artist must also struggle with the constraints of his and her own personality. As such, the struggle is not simply one of solving a technical puzzle, for example which colors do I mix in order to get this shade of green? But, rather, it is also a struggle for a vision that is inextricably, intrinsically spiritual. This can be clearly seen in Poulin's *Christmas Night at the Hermitage.*

Christmas Night at the Hermitage

The Hermitage of New Camaldoli is found on the hills facing the beautiful California coastline of Big Sur. The location of the Hermitage in the natural beauty of Big Sur is intentional. The Camaldolese, like all monks, recognize in the natural beauty of their surroundings the origins of their own spiritual journey. Contemplation of natural beauty leads the monk ever deeper into the depths of the human spirit. It is as if in the beauty of nature, the monk finds something of himself, a beauty that belongs to the depths of his humanity. For Fr. Poulin such contemplation strikes up the fire of his creativity, a creativity made possible not only in the hermit life but in participating in the common, shared memories of his community. As such, Poulin has developed an artistic style that is quite unique.

Perhaps, what strikes the viewer at first in *Christmas Night* is the technique used in the painting. Some have compared Poulin's technique with pointillism and impressionism but he doesn't see it that way. Pointillism aims at putting two colors together so that they "vibrate" and create a flat painting. His "points," on the other hand, are brushstrokes and are textured and many layered. He sums up his technique as "the one makes up the many." It is a "weaving," balancing approach to painting. His approach is different. "You know Alex," he said to me, "all of life begins with one dot." Each brushstroke for him is like the mustard seed, with the potential to explode. The "dot" is very special to him, "very powerful." It is the potentiality implied in the "dot," the potential to blossom into this unified whole like the "mustard seed," that strikes Arthur Poulin as powerful. For Poulin, his paintings begin with this hope implicit in the mustard seed, that is, the hope that when you plant it, it will grow.[5]

Indeed, Poulin begins every work by painting layer after layer of black gesso until an image begins to emerge. The process reminds him of Michelangelo's own process. Michelangelo felt that his job was not the making of an image but the releasing of an image already there in the marble. It reminds me of the ascetic process of the hermit that intends to empty the self of all desires and images so that God begins to fill the emptiness with images that transcend the resources of the hermit. Black gesso for Poulin is also symbolic of creativity. He doesn't make it easy on himself. He sees every painting as a spiritual journey and he has to respect the creative process as such and let it unfold as he journeys with it. In fact, his final work is often very different from his original intention. Art, he finds, is a revelation to the artist himself. Something from deep down inside is expressing itself. As such, art, he feels, is a burden and a responsibility. In the early stages of a painting, the faith dimension predominates where one hopes for things unseen. As such, it is the burden of the prophet, the giving birth to something new. In this artistic process, he sees the embodiment of Meister Eckhart's description of the mystical experience: "If the soul wants to know something about itself, it projects itself out, and then enters its projected self."[6]

Poulin finds his artistic creativity emerging not only from his solitary struggles with the interior life but also from the common life he shares with his Camaldolese brothers. He finds the Camaldolese tradition to be exceptionally open to artists. In their approach to the contemplative life lies a great openness to the nonverbal, to the message of the "image," indeed, a willingness to enter the "soul" of images. In St. Romuald's rule for the Camaldolese, the central message for the hermit is to "sit in your cell as in Paradise." For Arthur, every painting is about potential, a return to Paradise, that union of opposites with which every painting must struggle. The opposites of light and dark, warm and cold, lines and curves result in a creative tension in which the artist finds himself involved in various struggles. One can find himself blocked or resisting what the tension is spiritually trying to communicate. The aim of the artist is to work with that tension in order to restore that original unity where all those pieces fit. It is as returning to that first day of Creation. The artist is co-creating and can almost sense that delight God had in creating the universe.

Christmas Night at the Hermitage is an example of this spiritual journey. It was inspired by watching the heavens above the hermitage on a cool Christmas night, i.e., the night of the feast of the Incarnation. His feelings at the time were of something manifesting itself to the earth and the earth, responding, reaching out to this manifestation. This manifestation was essentially one of light and the painting is about light and darkness. "It is a night painting, a dark painting, full of purples, blues, and blacks." As such, he wanted the painting to manifest both a transparency to and the appearance of a marvelous, warm and embracing light even in the coolness of the dark colors of the night. Thus, he added warm colors, red and orange, to the sky in order to project that feeling of "warmth" he felt as he looked at the sky on Christmas night. Indeed, the entire composition is one of warm invitation and embrace. The coastline curves towards the night sky as an arm embraces a loved one. There is a continuity between the night sky and fertile, open earth. Arthur saw the painting as one of the Word becoming flesh, the ocean as a womb receptive and maternal to the light from the night sky. The trees are "looking," pointing to the stars. And the hermitage is painted in such a way as to be continuous with the trees.

The perspective in the painting suggests the Incarnation. Arthur deliberately chose the perspective of an icon as opposed to the classical rules of perspective. The perspective of the icon suggests interiority and depth. I am struck, however, in how one feels both as if looking down on the hermitage from a position above in the night sky and yet, at the same time, also looking at the night sky as from a position on the earth below. In any case, the painting suggests to the theologian a reflection on the meaning of the Incarnation. Moreover, the painting explores an often overlooked dimension of the Incarnation. Poulin's painting suggests that part of the meaning of the human nature of Christ is about recollecting the joy of the Earth.

The beauty of Fr. Poulin's paintings emerges from his own personal spirituality, a spirituality that is nourished and formed by his monastic community. As such, it appears to be a direct opposite of Duchamp's "spirituality." Duchamp is also involved in a spiritual struggle of sorts. He is trying to find the ultimate expression of artistic freedom. Such freedom Duchamp finds in the arbitrary aesthetic judgment of the artist. Poulin's artistic freedom is of a different sort. There is nothing arbitrary to the freedom present in Arthur's artistic style. Poulin's style is the product of a thousand-year-long communal tradition that has formed his sensibilities and spiritual life. It may seem like a paradox but Fr. Poulin's artistic freedom emerges from another greater freedom. To get at this paradox, we must take a look at the nature of the community that formed him and taught him a greater kind of freedom.

The Camaldolese: Hermits and Community

I wear a medal given to me by the Camaldolese when I became one of their oblates. The medal depicts an ancient image found in the mosaics of Ravenna, Italy. Two peacocks drink from the same cup. The cup appears to be liturgical and may be a eucharistic chalice. The two peacocks drinking from the same cup give vision to the Camaldolese belief that monastic life in community and monastic life in seclusion are not opposites of one another but nourish and sustain one another. Indeed, this was one of the great reforms that St. Romuald (ca. 950–1027) brought to monastic life in the eleventh century.[7] Up to the time of St. Romuald, two great monastic traditions, the anchorites (solitary life) and the cenobites (community life), had ambiguous and, at times, rocky relations with one another. The great hermitage tradition, the anchorites of Egypt, exalted the solitary search for purity of heart with a certain ambivalence to the common life.[8] The great cenobitic tradition exemplified in the Rule of Saint Benedict exalts the common life although it allows for the possibility of solitary life.[9] In both cases, the relation of one way of spiritual life with another remains ambiguous. St. Romuald, unfortunately, experienced the worst extremes of each kind of life.

St. Romuald, born from a noble family in Ravenna, originally joined the monastic communal way of life at the Abbey of St. Apollinaris in Classe in order to do penance for his father who had killed a man in a duel.[10] His stay at the monastery proved to be disastrous. Community life at the St. Apollinaris had grown lax and Romuald's attempts to reform it resulted in a plot by the monks to kill him. After three years at Classe, Romuald asked permission from his abbot to leave and was readily accommodated. He left Classe and sailed up the Adriatic coast to Cuxa, a place northeast of Venice. There he placed himself under the direction of a "holy eccentric" named Marinus. Marinus lived in complete solitude and Romuald spent three years with him. In those three years, Romuald realized that the absolute solitude of Marinus' spiritual life lacked a certain vigor or fecundity.[11]

Luckily, fate intervened. Peter Orseolo, the Doge of Venice, had a spiritual conversion and wanted to become a monk. He went to the hermitage of Marinus and Romuald to gain their advice. Together, they all decided to move to the famous Abbey of St. Michael in the Eastern Pyrenees mountains of Catalonia, Spain. This abbey, in addition to its community of monks, also hosted a colony of hermits on its grounds. At Cuxa, St. Romuald saw that the common life and the solitary life needed and sustained each other. With this insight, St. Romuald formulated his monastic reform. Monastic life is to have a warm, open spirit to the various forms of monastic experience, solitary (eremitic), common (cenobitic), and, even, missionary. This openness to the plurality of monastic life was called the "Threefold Good," and it has proven to be a powerful charism of the Camaldolese.

Indeed, the Camaldolese have contributed a number of individuals that have had a great influence not only on the Church but on Western society in general. Thus, the Camaldolese can count as one of their own, Gratian (d. ca. 1179), who has been called the "father of canon law." Dante, in fact, mentions Gratian along with Romuald and Peter Damian as being in Paradise. Another great Camaldolese was Fra Mauro (d. 1459), the great cartologist whose pioneering charts helped Columbus in his journeys. Perhaps more relevant to our subject are the great artists that emerged from the Camaldolese community. Guido of Arezzo (d. 1050), for example, has been called the "father of modern music." In order to help the monks chant the psalms more effectively, he devised a system of staff lines and notes that became the model for our modern musical notation. Even more pertinent, Lorenzo Monaco (d. ca. 1424), who was perhaps the most important Florentine artist of the early fifteenth century, had great influence on the Dominican artist Fra Angelico.

Purity of Heart

The Camaldolese charism, then, is a warm, open spirit full of creative energy. This creative energy somehow comes about in the interaction between the individual's struggle with the interior life and the community's struggle with its common life both open to the demands of the world outside the community. This combination of solitary quest, common life, and missionary openness is the reason why a hermit artist might give us insights into the relationship between artistic creativity and artistic freedom. The Camaldolese hermit is not some rugged individual trying to avoid community life or the world outside. He finds sustenance and nourishment for his solitary journey in the community that prays with and for him in the context of a world in dire need of spiritual direction. In turn, the Camaldolese hermit nourishes and sustains the community by sharing the fruits of his own struggle with the interior life.

Sharing the fruits of a spiritual struggle is a far cry from the constant innovation demanded by aesthetic nominalism. Indeed, Mary Carruthers in her groundbreaking book, *The Craft of Thought,* points out that "the notions of what constitutes 'inventio' have changed significantly from the small-group societies of the pre-modern West to the rationalist individualism of the nineteenth century."[12] The Latin word *inventio* has two meanings. The first meaning is what we ordinarily mean by "invention," that is the "creation of something new." The other meaning, however, is "inventory," or "the storage of many diverse materials." This second meaning of *inventio* involved the "art of memory." In other words, creative thinking was more than pure novelty; it meant creating new meaning out of the memories of a community. *Inventio* was a craft highly developed by the monks for the purposes of "forming citizens of the City of God." In their common chanting of the psalms and the reading of the Fathers, the monks kept alive a tradition not as a museum of antiquities but as a resource for "inventing" a vibrant, living interpretation of their tradition, a tradition often challenged by the world brought to their hermitage steps. Indeed, Carruthers gives as an example of *inventio,* St. Romuald's rule for the Camaldolese.[13] What Carruthers' study of creative thinking and its relation to memory affords a theology of art is the affirmation that artistic creativity does not emerge from an unbridled freedom emerging out of some absolute subjectivity but that artistic freedom finds its energy in the individual's struggle with the interior life participating in the common interpretation of shared memories in the face of a difficult and uncertain future. Indeed, creative thinking concerns religious insight, the close and personal knowledge of the need of salvation and the quest into the way of salvation.

Yet *inventio* does not quite describe the source of the Camaldolese creative energy. *Inventio,* as such, describes the process of monastic creativity but it does not of itself tell us where it is found. It is in St. Romuald's rule that we find a clue. St. Romuald tells us to "sit in your cell as in Paradise." What St. Romuald is alluding to is the monk's ultimate aim. This aim is well expressed in John Cassian's writings of the desert hermit monks: "every love, every desire, every effort, every undertaking, every thought of ours, everything that we live, that we speak, that we breathe, will be God . . . and that unity which the Father now has with the Son and which the Son has with the Father will be carried over into our minds and senses."[14] Such blissful union of human and Divine freedoms is what the monastic tradition refers to as a "return to Paradise." As such, it is only possible, John Cassian tells us, through purity of heart. The "pure of heart" refers to the heart as a source of vision characterized by sincerity, tranquility, integrity of purpose.[15] Purity of heart is "that practice of holiness described as love or perfection or contemplation or tranquility" in Cassian's *Conferences.*[16] Indeed, purity of heart is another dimension of "a wounded innocence."

Purity of heart, as this wounded innocence, is the reason hermits go into the desert or into reclusion. "There is a depth within the human being and within nature that can only be explored in solitude."[17] As such, purity of heart unlocks the vision the heart is possible of making, the creativity it is capable of generating. Purity of heart is the condition of true vision but it comes at a price. Purity of heart does not come for those who know nothing of spiritual struggle. Purity of heart comes to be as the result of long and arduous spiritual struggle. It is, I think, the condition for true human freedom and, thus, true creativity. It is the condition for that kind of vision that Maritain describes as "what's left to us of Paradise." As such, purity of heart is a crucial ingredient of true artistic creativity and a key dimension of "a wounded innocence."

Sit in Your Cell as in Paradise

Here, then, lies a spiritual dimension proper to the work of art. It is experience of the spiritual struggle of human freedom towards self-transcendence made visible in the work of art that began in a solitary journey, a journey, however, sustaining and sustained, nourishing and nourished in community. I began this chapter exploring the nature of artistic creativity. I noted at the time that the theological dimension of artistic creativity emerged in the relationship between human freedom and Divine Freedom. The question of the possibility of human self-transcendence now takes us into this relationship. For the question of human self-transcendence now queries the resources of human freedom for such a project. Can human freedom alone suffice for human self-transcendence? The Christian answer is "No." However, human freedom nourished, sustained by and fulfilled in God's own freedom can. This is the revelation given to us in the Incarnation. Jesus, in his human freedom, obedient to his Father's Will, opened up the possibility of human self-transcendence not in a human freedom that is blind, not in a human freedom that knows no other freedom but itself, but in a human freedom which keeps in sight a larger freedom that is divine.

Such sight of a larger freedom, such vision of uniting a lesser with a greater freedom, defines as well the theological dimension of the issue of iconoclasm. For iconoclasm, in the ultimate theological analysis, is blindness to the awesome freedom of God. Whether such blindness manifests itself in a fear of images or despair over the possibility of human self-transcendence, iconoclasm is the antithesis of human creativity for it lacks the resources for self-transcendence. The iconoclast can never be surprised by God's unpredictable, incommensurate, gracious freedom for it is blind to God's creativity as well. And God's creativity, as the tradition points out, is the ultimate source of our own human creativity. Fr. Poulin's *Christmas Sky* exemplifies the best of human creativity for it is a journey that amounts to openness to a larger freedom. From his black gesso to his aesthetic appreciation of a cold, Christmas night, Fr. Poulin kept in sight the larger freedom that guided, indeed, incarnated, his artistic creativity. Such vision is the result of his own spiritual struggles, struggles that cultivate purity of heart, the condition crucial for true creativity.

Art's true beauty is not simply the pleasure it gives but, insofar as it gives witness to the spiritual struggle to truly see, it also affirms the goodness of our humanity nourishing the hope that someday human evil shall be transcended and "all tears will be wiped away." Indeed, Poulin's painting, in its beauty and spirituality, allows this spiritually struggling oblate to fulfill St. Romuald's rule to "sit in your cell as in Paradise."

1. Thomas Matus, Peter Damian, and Bruno, *The Mystery of Romuald and the Five Brothers: Stories from the Benedictines and Camaldolese* (Trabuco Canyon, Calif.: Source Books, 1994) 66.

2. For a contemporary discussion see Ned Bustard, *It Was Good Making Art to the Glory of God* (Baltimore, Md.: Square Halo Books, 2000) 191–93.

3. John Paul II, "Letter to Artists," *Origins* 28, no. 46 (1999) 787.

4. Ibid.

5. Alex García-Rivera, personal conversation, interview with Arthur Poulin, O.S.B. Cam. (Incarnation Monastery, 2001). The rest of this section is based on this personal interview.

6. Poulin attributes this image to Eckhart. Hegel, however, also has a similar account. See, e.g., Georg Wilhelm Friedrich Hegel, Bernard Bosanquet, and M. J. Inwood, *Introductory Lectures on Aesthetics,* edited by M. J. Inwood, translated by Bernard Bosanquet, Penguin Classics (London/New York: Penguin Books, 1993) 36.

7. In one sense, it is not accurate to call St. Romuald a "founder" of a religious order. The Camaldolese do not see themselves entirely as a religious order or a school of spirituality. Their self-understanding reaches back to the earliest monks of both East and West to the point that Camaldolese believe that "there is something of the monk in every person, a kind of universal monastic archetype." Robert Hale, O.S.B. Cam., "Camaldolese Spirituality," in *The New Dictionary of Catholic Spirituality,* edited by Michael Downey (Collegeville, Minn.: The Liturgical Press, 1993) 107.

8. Cassian's *Conferences* gives an example of this. At the beginning of the *Conferences,* Cassian sees the common (cenobitic) monastic life as independently separate from the solitary (anchoritic) monastic life of his fellow Egyptian monks. By the end of the *Conferences,* however, he softens this judgment by admitting that the common monastic life can help sustain and enrich the solitary monastic life. Nonetheless, this judgment into the relationship between cenobitic and anchoritic life remains somewhat ambiguous. John Cassian and Boniface Ramsey, *John Cassian, The Conferences,* translated by Boniface Ramsey, Ancient Christian Writers (New York: Paulist Press, 1997) 23.

9. Robert Hale, O.S.B. Cam., "Eremitical Life," in *The New Dictionary of Catholic Spirituality,* edited by Michael Downey (Collegeville, Minn.: The Liturgical Press, 1993) 353.

10. A fine account of Romuald's life can be found in Matus, Peter Damian, and Bruno, op. cit. For a brief but informative account of the Camaldolese community in general see Lino Vigilucci, *Camaldoli: A Journey into Its History & Spirituality* (Trabuco Canyon, Calif.: Source Books Hermitage Books, 1995).

11. Vigilucci, op. cit., 36.

12. Mary Carruthers, *The Craft of Thought Meditation, Rhetoric, and the Making of Images, 400–1200,* Cambridge Studies in Medieval Literature (New York: Cambridge University Press, 1998) 10.

13. Ibid., 112.

14. Cassian and Ramsey, op. cit., 10.7.2.

15. J. Lambrecht, S.J., "Beatitudes," in *The New Dictionary of Catholic Spirituality,* edited by Michael Downey (Collegeville, Minn.: The Liturgical Press, 1993) 81–82.

16. Cassian and Ramsey, op. cit., 19.

17. Hale, "Eremitical Life," 352.

“The ‘Anagogical’ Window”

CHAPTER FOUR

Heaven-with-Us

The Stained-Glass Windows of St-Denis

An icon immediately brings to mind the religious art of the Eastern Byzantine Church. In contrast, the stained-glass window is what immediately brings to mind Western Christian art. Both kinds of art captured complex and profound theological systems in a single visual stroke. In a sense, the difference between these two kinds of art lies in the difference between Athens and Rome. Athens and Rome provided the cultural substrates out of which the community of faith made their works of art. Hellenic art concentrated on images, that is making realistic copies of an original. Theirs was an art trying to imitate the cosmos. Roman art, on the other hand, concentrated on *istoria,* that is, on telling a story. The Romans loved to write stories of their victories on columns and arches.

Christian art is not identical with either Hellenic or Roman art but possesses characteristics of both. Indeed, Christian art consists of both images and *istoria.* Early Christian art tended to the Hellenic preference for images.[1] Nonetheless, those images were part of the stories from the Old and New Testaments. As Christianity moved into the West, the Roman preference for narrative began to exert more influence and Christian art entered a new phase. It began to be used and understood in terms of Roman rhetoric. At the same time, Eastern Christianity began to increasingly emphasize the image as a model of Christian art. Thus, early Christian art began to evolve into two different forms as the Church began to spread from Constantinople and Rome.

At the same time, a significant challenge emerged for Christian art. Iconoclasm enveloped Eastern Byzantium with winds of fury. For the East, iconoclasm became, literally, a life-and-death struggle for the soul of the Church. From the struggle emerged Christological doctrines which were formalized in a variety of creeds and council decrees.[2] For the West, iconoclasm did not prove to be so traumatic. Nonetheless, it also raised a series of serious theological challenges. In the East, the issue involved the possibility of making a copy of a divine original. In the West, however, the issue involved the possibility of seeing the invisible by means of the visible. What Eastern iconoclasm challenged was the possibility of God-with-us. What Western iconoclasm challenged was the possibility of "Heaven-with-us." Heaven-with-us meant the possibility of seeing the spiritually invisible through the materially visible. Heaven-with-us also meant standing at that threshold between this world and the world to come. As such, Heaven-with-us also means the eschatological dimension of the kingdom of God.

Heaven-with-us was the artistic (and theological) aim of the stained-glass window. It offered the beholder a very special sensibility, a spiritual vision, to the world of Heaven almost-at-hand yet always-beyond-reach. Such spiritual vision sanctified the beholder. In this chapter, I take a look at Western medieval art in the form of the Gothic cathedral and its stained-glass windows. Perhaps the best example of the artistic and theological aspirations of the period is the so-called "Anagogical" window commissioned for the Abbey of St-Denis by Abbot Suger. The "Anagogical" window, indeed, the whole abbey provides a rich resource for a reflection on the nature of religious art, for in its conception and achievement, it managed to put into visual form an entire metaphysical and theological system and make it accessible to the uneducated and illiterate of the Church.

The stained-glass window of Western Christian art shows how closely tied theology and the arts can be. An important insight, I believe, will come out of this reflection. Religious art, in a deep sense, not only concerns itself with divine presence but also concerns itself in making present the reality of heaven. In other words, religious art contains a profound eschatological dimension. For the Gothic West, religious art became a *porta caeli,* a "gate of heaven," in which the world-to-come became present. Moreover, this took place by evoking a wonderful sensibility, a "spiritual vision," which gave the beholder the aesthetic experience of a "higher" and a "lower." As such, the "spiritual vision" at the "gate" of heaven became a sanctifying experience. The evoking of "spiritual vision," however, takes place only in the open soil of a *wounded innocence.*

A Subtle Shift

Peter Brown identifies a noticeable shift in Christian art in the passage from late antiquity into the medieval age. The art of the Middle

Ages began to emphasize less the experience of participation than a bridge to a "higher" spiritual world, less the experience of art as a "window" to the divine than a "bridge" to the spiritually invisible God. As Brown puts it,

> from a specifically late antique "period eye" to one that will become more dominant in the early middle ages—a shift, perhaps, from participation to vision. We begin with an art . . . that did justice to the yearning of the late antique Christians to find themselves surrounded by a *mundus* transformed. We end with a wish for clear "windows" on to another world, such as could only be provided by a carefully-codified array of visual representations. And these windows look on to a Paradise where nature and the animal world, though present, have sunk into the background. Paradise, the "garden of delights," now takes second place to the precise outlines of the human face. . . . After 700 A.D., it had become a little more possible for Christians to enter churches . . . plucked by a sharp sense of worlds held at a distance from us . . . of worlds inhabited by the holy dead, made present, on earth, by the silent faces on the icons and by the quiet, charged gestures of narrative scenes. We should be careful not to expect this particular sensibility in earlier centuries of Christianity.[3]

What Brown suggests is that a subtle but important shift began to take place around A.D. 700 with respect to Christian art. The redemptive immediacy early Christian art offered in the form of communion with divine presence began to shift towards a more mediated, interpretive offer of divine presence. Redemptive immediacy became sanctifying vision.

Brown does not suggest that this was a paradigm shift in Christian art history. Rather, the development is due to a variety of theological issues that took Western Christian art on a different path than Eastern Byzantine art. One of these issues was the role of images in the faith of the poor and illiterate. Serenus, bishop of Marseilles about the year 600, destroyed (or, at least, was reported to have destroyed) all the religious images in the churches of his city. Pope Gregory the Great, hearing of this, sent him a letter that would be quoted time and time again in the Church's self-understanding of the role religious art plays in the life of the Church. Gregory wrote Serenus: "It is one thing to worship a painting, and quite another to learn from a scene represented in a painting what ought to be worshiped. For what writing provides for people who read, paintings provide for the illiterate *(idiotis)* who look at them, since these unlearned people see what they must imitate;

paintings are books for those who do not know their letters, so that they take the place of books specially among pagans."[4]

With these words, Pope Gregory articulated the basic justifying principle for the Western Church's relationship to visual arts: they are the *libri idiotarum,* the books of the illiterate.[5] Through this principle, Pope Gregory made clear three important aims of Christian art. First, art aids in instructing the faithful, specially the unlettered who can learn from visual imagery as if from books. Second, art acts as an aid to memory so that the mysteries of the Scriptures and the Church become firmly fixed in the hearts who see them every time they walk into the church or cathedral. Finally, art inculcates more effectively devotion since it engages the senses much more effectively than words engage the mind.[6]

Western Christian art now began a subtle shift. At the heart of Gregory's justifications was the Church's esteem of Roman rhetoric. In Gregory's eyes, art's greatest gift is its ability to persuade. As Besançon puts it: "The image fortifies, edifies the faithful, it touches their intelligence, their feelings *(componctio),* their memories, that is, their "selves," in the sense the ancients gave that word. The image is rhetorical in the strong sense. It persuades, it instructs, it moves, it pleases, it counsels (deliberative mode), it accuses or defends (legal mode), it praises or blames (epideictic mode): the categories of Ciceronian rhetoric perfectly applied to Gregory's program."[7] Gregory had given art a new dimension: Roman rhetoric. This rhetorical view had subtle consequences on the art that followed.

Western Christian art now began to take on the dignity of sacred writing as opposed to sacred object. As such, Western Christian art lent itself to a greater openness than was possible with the rigid specifications required of the Eastern icon. Indeed, Western Christian art became fertile with subjects and forms not specifically Christian. Western Christian art aimed less at direct representation than persuading one to lead a devoted and virtuous Christian life. Thus, Western Christian art's rhetorical basis allowed a tremendous freedom of expression and a certain appreciation of all art. Such great openness, however, also opened it to secular forces that one day would compromise its religious reason for being.[8]

If nothing else, Gregory's rhetorical justifying principle offered an important insight into the nature of religious art. Just like the words of Scripture must be interpreted, art too must be interpreted. But is interpreting art the same as interpreting text? Theologians of the period realized that there were similarities but also differences. Interpreting a scriptural passage and a work of art have similarities. Interpreting a scriptural text often meant looking elsewhere than its literal meaning. When Scripture portrays God as a "shepherd," it does not mean for us to understand God literally as a "shepherd." The same can be said for a religious work of art. For art, "literalness" means the physical art object itself. Interpreting a religious work beyond the "literal" means looking beyond the physical work itself onto a deeper, spiritual meaning or, as Dewey might have put it, to a wholeness of experience greater than oneself.

There are, however, differences. Interpreting a work of art is more than an intellectual act, a hermeneutics of text. Hermeneutics is a fairly cerebral process that involves linguistic, source, textual, historical, and cultural analysis. In contrast, interpreting religious art involves the inextricable engagement of both emotions and the intellect. Such interpretation involves both analysis and synthesis yet it is neither. For weeping can be a valid "interpretation" of a work of art. As such, weeping engages the entire individual, mind, heart, and soul. It is not simply a mind interpreting a work. In a sense, in the interpretation of a work of art, it is less the beholder that interprets the art but the art that interprets the beholder.

Aesthetic interpretation, indeed, differs greatly from hermeneutical interpretation. Theologians of the period understood the process in the following way. A religious work of art evokes feelings that cannot be satisfied by the "literal" work of art itself and, thus, the beholder begins to search for the true object of longing. That true object of longing was defined according to the theology of Pseudo-Dionysius about whom I shall say more later in this chapter. For now, let it suffice to say that Dionysius saw all beings in the world participating in the Divine One through ladder-like cascade of light emerging from the One and, thus, also returning to the One. What Dionysius proposed was an interconnected hierarchy of beings in which beauty was experienced as the spiritual movement from a "lower" to a "higher."[9] This spiritual movement was also ontological. The experience of a "higher" from a "lower" also brought to the beholder a "being more." As such, interpreting a work of art also becomes a process of sanctification.

Art, so considered, makes the artistic challenge evident. First, the artist must engage the emotions of the beholder. Indeed, one of the main characteristics of Gothic art is the exquisite animation and expressiveness of its figures. Such expressiveness was achieved by emphasizing deformity or strange hybrids of creatures as well as skill in animating expression in its subjects.[10] The expressiveness of these medieval craftsmen was such that St. Bernard would protest:

> But apart from this, in the cloisters, before the eyes of the brothers while they read—what is this ridiculous monstrosity doing, an amazing kind of deformed beauty and yet a beautiful deformity? What are the filthy apes doing here? The fierce lions? The monstrous centaurs? The creatures, part man and beast? The striped tigers? The fighting soldiers? The hunters blowing horns? You may see many bodies under one head, and conversely many heads on one body. On one side the tail of a serpent is seen on a quadruped, on the other side the head of a quadruped is on the body of a fish. Over there an animal has a horse for the front half and a goat for the back; here a creature which is horned in front is equine behind. In short, everywhere so plentiful and astonishing a variety of contradictory forms is seen that one would rather read in the marble than in books, and spend the whole day wondering at every single one of them than in meditating on the law of God.[11]

St. Bernard, in a sense, pointed out the true challenge for the artist of Gothic art. There is a sort of paradox to the aesthetic aim of the medieval work of art. The power of such art depends on its ability to engage the senses. Nevertheless, the dynamics of engagement depends on the work calling attention to its own sensuality. Thus, the work of art itself can co-opt the quest for a "higher" spiritual end and easily become the actual object of longing. The artistic challenge, then, consists in effectively engaging the senses in such a way as to point them beyond the physical attractiveness of the work of art itself.

Medieval artists did this in a variety of ways. They began to animate their figures with great expressiveness.[12] By aiming for greater lifelikeness and choosing subjects such as monsters or strange, deformed creatures, medieval artists hoped to engage the senses more effectively. Bernard's monstrosities were not simply whimsies of an artist's imagination. They were intentionally monstrous in order to keep the senses from dwelling on them. Similarly, human subjects were made intentionally unattractive, even, downright ugly, in order to urge the senses not to dwell on the "literal" subject but seek a "higher," more spiritual end. These are negative elements, however.

Medieval artists also possessed positive methods to guide the senses towards the spiritual. Greatest of these was their craftsman skill. It is hard to realize today but artists in this period were not seen as "artists" but as craftsmen. It was not until the Renaissance that artists began to see their vocation as other than craftsmanship. In any case, the medieval artist depended on the beauty of his skill to compete with the beauty of the material elements of his work. Thus, the heart would be attracted more by the beauty of the invisible skill than the beauty of the visible material. It is in this period that one begins to see the aesthetic value of a work of art associated with the skill of the artist. In the Renaissance, the value of skill will take enormous significance.[13]

Abbot Suger and the Abbey of St-Denis

It should come as no surprise that the thought of Pseudo-Dionysius played a great role in the artistic inspiration for the architecture and the windows of the Abbey of St-Denis. The Abbey of St-Denis was esteemed above all other sacred places in France because it held the relics of St-Denis. St-Denis converted France to Christianity in the third century and, thus, was known as the "Apostle of France." St-Denis, however, was also believed to be Dionysius (or Denis), the Areopagite, the convert of Mars' hill (and a disciple of Paul) mentioned in Acts 17.[14] This Dionysius, or Denis, was also believed to have written *On the Divine Names,* and *The Celestial Hierarchy.* These works had recently entered the medieval West and enjoyed popularity due to the translation and commentary of such intellectual figures such as John Scot Eurigena and Hugh of St. Victor. Today, we know that Dionysius did not write these works (thus the Pseudo used to refer to this Dionysius). In the Middle Ages, however, Dionysius was uncritically acknowledged to have written these great treatises on light, the universe, and participation in the One. Who exactly wrote *The Celestial Hierarchy* and *The Divine Names* did not matter to the ordinary faithful. Pilgrims streamed to the Abbey of St-Denis to venerate the great disciple of Paul and apostle to France now resting within the abbey's doors.[15]

The significance of the abbey and its architecture cannot be measured without understanding the life and motivation of its greatest abbot, Suger. Suger was born into a family of quite modest means in 1080 or 1081 at Chennevères-lès-Louvres, a village about ten miles from the abbey. When he was ten years old, he was received by the monks of the abbey as an oblate. Suger flourished at the abbey and soon rose in prominence. By the time he was twenty-five years of age, the abbey entrusted him with many missions. In 1112, he was sent as a delegate to the Lateran Council. Since St-Denis was the royal abbey, he soon came to know King Louis VI. He became St-Denis' abbot on March 12, 1122. As abbot, Suger enjoyed the trust and confidence of his monks as well as of the king. Nonetheless, he was faced with a history of a loosely run monastery and an abbey that had fallen into disrepair.[16]

These twin problems offered a difficult challenge. Suger had to increase the discipline in his abbey while at the same time begin a campaign to repair and remodel the abbey. These two goals were, in a sense, at odds with each other. Monastic reform called for a return to strict observance of voluntary poverty and simplicity of life. Rebuilding the abbey meant seeking money and dealing with worldly trades. In doing this, Suger occasioned the wrath of the great monastic reformer, Bernard of Clairvaux. Bernard's call to monastic reform put into even harsher light Suger's twin challenges. Bernard's reforms called for reclusion, self-mortification, austerity, and simplicity. These values, though valid for a monastic ideal, are at odds for a place meant for multitudes of pilgrims. Nonetheless, Bernard criticized Suger with devastating rhetoric.

In this, Bernard did theology of art a great favor. He forced Suger to articulate a theology of art to counter his critique. In other words, Bernard forced Suger to give spiritual justification for bringing beauty into a place meant for the mortification of one's soul. For Suger, like Gregory the Great, that justification found its reason in the spirituality of the largely unlettered lay people. St-Denis, after all, was a pilgrimage site. While learned monks had access to spiritual realities through inspired writings, the illiterate peasants did not. St-Denis would become a place where *"de materialibus ad immaterialia excitans"* (that is "the material takes us into the immaterial"). These words, taken from Suger's own account of the rebuilding of St-Denis *(De Administratione),* are also a summary of the theology of Pseudo-Dionysius.[17] These words, however, are better "seen" than "read." This, Suger did, with his stained-glass windows.

The Theological Aesthetics of St-Denis

The stained-glass windows of Suger's abbey embody an exquisite theology of light. There are three theological themes crucial to understanding St-Denis' theological aesthetics. One of these elements is Augustine's reflections on light. In his commentary on Genesis, *De Genesi ad Litteram,* Augustine reflected on the meaning of the words "Fiat lux" ("And light was made") and brought into the theological tradition a perennial interest in the theology of light and of vision.[18] Augustine notes that light was the first creature made out of "nothing." As the "first incarnation" of God's Word, light is the supreme example of God's beauty or form.[19] Moreover, since light is incorporeal, it is the most spiritual of all "creatures." And since light is not only incorporeal but also visible, it is the ultimate mediator between the visible and the invisible, the material and the immaterial.

Augustine also provided the second theological element of St-Denis' theological aesthetics. In *De Genesi Ad Litteram* he describes the kind of vision the blessed will have of God at the end of time:

> The brightness of the Lord is seen, not through a symbolic or corporeal vision, as it was seen on Mount Sinai, nor through a spiritual vision such as Isaiah saw and John in the Apocalypse, but through a direct vision and not through a dark image, as far as the human mind elevated by the Grace of God can receive it. In such a vision God speaks face to face to him whom He has made worthy of this communion. And here we are speaking not of the face of the body but of that of the mind.[20]

Augustine here suggests the crux of the theology that would dominate Western Christian art. It is not invisibility that is an obstacle to representing God. It is the need for a new kind of vision altogether. Such vision would be quite different from the physical vision used to see the visible, material things of this world. Augustine called it "intellectual vision."[21]

If Augustine had left it at that, then Western iconoclasm would have won the day. "Intellectual vision," after all would only be ours at the end of time. Augustine, however, continued his reflections on vision, indicating that a third type of vision is yet possible for us. Augustine called this third type of vision, "spiritual vision." "Spiritual vision" is possible because "when we come into contact with a body by means of our bodily senses . . . the image of it is immediately formed in our spirit and stored in our memory."[22] As such, "spiritual vision" is a bridge between the corporal, physical vision of this world and the "intellectual vision" of the world to come. Augustine's "spiritual vision" puts the one who has it with one foot in this world and the other in the world to come.

The third, and most elaborate, element of Suger's theological aesthetics is the theology of Pseudo-Dionysius. Pseudo-Dionysius borrowed heavily from Neoplatonic thought and the Gospel of John.[23] All being emanates from God, the One. Because all creatures emanate from the One, a type of analogy can be made. All creatures participate in some way in the very Being of their Creator. As such, they are, in various degrees, images, symbols, or mirrors of God. Since light, however, is the principal form or "mirror" of God, then the aesthetic value of a creature depends to the degree it partakes of light.[24] Since light dims the further away it is from its source, such participation creates a hierarchy or "ladder" of participation. Thus, in Pseudo-Dionysius' system, all material realities have a corresponding spiritual dimension, a "spiritual vision" of an aspect of God. This vision, however, was an "interpretation," for material realities by virtue of their analogical participation in the One are also symbols, and symbols must be interpreted. The interpretation that is a vision had a name. It is what Pseudo-Dionysius called "anagogy."

"Anagogy" is a Greek term for "uplifting," or "raised higher." It is the key theme of Pseudo-Dionysius' theology. Although, Pseudo-Dionysius goes to great length to describe anagogy, it is best described as a spiritual experience. Perhaps one of the best descriptions of this anagogical experience is a famous passage by Suger given in *De Administratione.*

> Thus, when—out of my delight in the beauty of the house of God—the loveliness of the many-colored gems has called me away from external cares, and worthy meditation has induced me to reflect, transferring that which is material to that which is immaterial, on the diversity of the sacred virtues: then it seems to me that I see myself dwelling, as it were, in some strange region of the universe which neither exists entirely in the slime of the earth nor entirely in the purity of Heaven; and that, by the grace of God, I can be transported from this inferior to that higher world in an anagogical manner.[25]

Anyone who has entered a quiet church in the middle of the day and knelt silently in the soft blue light from its windows knows what Suger is talking about. This spiritual "uplift" is the artistic embodiment of what Pseudo-Dionysius called anagogy.

"Porta Caeli"

Perhaps no greater synthesis of art and theology has been achieved than in the stained-glass windows of the Gothic cathedral. The windows are meant not simply to be looked at but to define the space within as sacred. They did this by combining the considerable spiritual qualities of light, the luminosity of color, and the intellectual qualities of a metaphysical system into an artistic and theological whole that is still breathtaking. The theology of light developed via Augustine and Pseudo-Dionysius was successfully visualized in the artistry of the windows. This theology changed the passive visual aesthetics that previous art had aimed at. The visual sensuality of the windows was meant less to be seen than to evoke a vision. This was the thrust of the entire Dionysian aesthetic and the basis for Augustine's "spiritual vision." Thus, the windows combined Augustine's understanding of light as the most spiritual of all creatures, Dionysius' anagogical experience of interpretation, and Augustine's third type of vision, that bridge between this world and the world to come into an experience that placed the beholder at the brink of heaven.

As such, the stained-glass windows of St-Denis are meant to be more than a work of art all by themselves. They take part in a whole system of artistic endeavor, a community of works of art that is the chapel of St-Denis. Indeed, Suger meant the aesthetics of St-Denis to be more than an appreciation of beauty. St-Denis was meant to be a vision, a "spiritual vision" of the world to come. This is made clear in the west entrance to the abbey chapel. The door itself is modeled after a Roman city gate. On the *tympanum* or top of the door, a scene of the Last Judgment and the resurrection of the dead is carved into the stone. Just as Augustine's "spiritual vision" was a bridge to the "intellectual" vision of the endtime, St-Denis would be a bridge, a "gate" to a vision of that end time, a *porta caeli,* a "gate of heaven." This was, in a sense, nothing more than a continuation of early Christian art that aimed to present a world transformed by the resurrection of Christ. The world transformed would now come closer via the "spiritual vision" afforded in the beauty of St-Denis.

This intention was made clear to the pilgrims that came by the thousands through its doors. Abbot Suger had his artist-craftsmen make a copper-gilt inscription that was on the door to the west entrance. Its message was inescapable:

> Whoever thou art, if thou seekest to extol the glory of these doors,
> Marvel not at the gold and the expense but at the craftsmanship of the work.
> Bright is the noble work; but, being nobly bright, the work
> Should brighten the minds, so that they may travel, through the true lights,
> To the True Light where Christ is the true door.
> In what manner it be inherent in this world the golden door defines:
> The dull mind rises to truth through that which is material
> And, in seeing this light, is resurrected from its former submersion.[26]

As such, this inscription was a guide for the pilgrim on how to behold the beauty they would find inside. It was, in a sense, the interpretive key, that is the "interpretant," for the experience of the art of St-Denis. As such, it told the pilgrim they were entering an intermediate place between the world to come and the world that is. The pilgrim was to prepare to enter the "gate of heaven."

In St-Denis, an important new theological insight into the theology of art was revealed. If the Eastern Byzantine iconoclast conflict revealed the Incarnation to be a major theological element in the theology of art, then St-Denis revealed that a theology of art also contained a profound eschatological dimension. Art was not only a "window" to the Divine but a "bridge" to the world-to-come. Indeed, when the pilgrim entered the Abbey of St-Denis the first impression most probably was one of a deep blue luminosity bathing the interior space of the cathedral. This deep blue luminosity was due to the *materia saphirorum,* that is sapphire-glass, present in the stained-glass windows. Although stained-glass windows existed in the Romanesque churches before Suger's Gothic reformation, Suger innovated the generous use of this sapphire-glass in his windows. The "Anagogical Window," for example, is an example of this generosity.

As such, Suger's stained-glass windows gave a deep blue luminosity to the interior space of the churches on which they were placed. Although many commentators emphasize the Gothic "gloom" of such deep blue luminosity, they fail to appreciate not only the theological dimension attempted by this "gloom" but also its artistic aim. One of the artistic aims of medieval Christian art was expressiveness. When the artist is dealing with sculpture, engravings, or paintings, expression is done through greater animation in the depiction of figures. But how does the artist bring expressiveness to light? Light, after all, does not have the materiality that sculpture or paintings have. Medieval artists discovered the expressiveness of light in its color. They used color to "animate" and make more expressive the light shining into the cathedral. This artistic insight ought to give a clue to the theological dimension of Suger's Gothic windows.

Not "gloom" but "twilight," is the aesthetic aim of that deep blue luminosity. "Twilight" blue refers to that region where earth meets the heavens. As such, the deep blue luminosity from the windows signifies a special vantage place in order to see the world and ourselves in a very special way. This vantage place evokes a kind of seeing that is not corporal vision that can only see the material things of this world. Neither does this kind of vision involve "intellectual vision" for it does not pretend to be the vision given only in the final Resurrection.

Rather, it is the vision for those of us that find our lives somewhere between the woundedness of this world and the wholesome vision of the next. It is vision for those of us wounded yet full of hope. It is vision that bridges the cares of this world and the joy of the next. It is "spiritual vision" that the deep blue luminosity of Gothic "twilight" aims to evoke. Almost all who experience this "twilight" region feel enabled with a special kind of vision. The material elements of the cathedral become transformed into Heaven-with-us and one feels quite naturally the urge to whisper.

Indeed, the "twilight" blue brings the beholder into visual contact with the heavens for the experience of "twilight" blue is meant to be the experience of Heaven-with-us. As such, the experience of Heaven-with-us also encompasses the twin elements of religious art, compassion, and sympathy. "Twilight" blue as the animation technique of the medieval artist was meant to engage the emotions. As such, the "twilight" blue luminosity of Suger's windows meant to engender a special type of compassion, a compassion for things spiritual, the things of heaven. Such compassion demands, however, a certain kind of innocence, an openness to the things of heaven. Whereas cynicism might only see "Gothic gloom," innocence sees all things hoped for. It is no coincidence, I believe, that Suger had the pilgrim in mind when he designed his abbey. The hope and aim of every pilgrim is that in his and her long journey, innocence is discovered anew. It is the innocence, however, of one who carries the woundedness of earthly burdens.

Thus, the pilgrim who gains compassion for the things of heaven is also the one who carries a burden of earthly sorrows. Such wounded innocence elicits divine sympathy. The love for the things of heaven calls for the love of heaven. Heaven-with-us means that compassion and divine sympathy become one in this in-between region of the "twilight" blue of St-Denis. As such, the "spiritual vision" of heaven afforded at St-Denis is more than a means to an end. Its uplifting is more than a "shot in the arm" for the weary pilgrim. The wounded innocent blessed with "spiritual vision" takes home a piece of that heaven. In other words, "spiritual vision" sanctifies. At St-Denis, the hoped-for future of the pilgrim interprets the tradition's past to his and her weary present in a way only eschatological presence can provide. Having experienced Heaven-with-us, the pilgrim leaves St-Denis with greater charity, higher hopes, and fortified faith. The pilgrim gains a new innocence to the things of heaven, and, thus, to the things of this world. Suger's Gothic achievement lies less in the novelty of a new kind of art, but in the achievement of an exquisitely intertwined theological truth and artistic skill. As such, Suger has revealed the color of a wounded innocence. It is deep twilight blue.

1. For noteworthy studies of early Christian art the reader may consult Paul Corby Finney, *The Invisible God: The Earliest Christians on Art* (New York: Oxford University Press, 1994); André Grabar, *Christian Iconography: A Study of Its Origins* (Princeton, N.J.: Princeton University Press, 1968); Robin Margaret Jensen, *Understanding Early Christian Art* (London/New York: Routledge, 2000); Thomas F. Mathews, *The Clash of Gods: A Reinterpretation of Early Christian Art* (Princeton, N.J.: Princeton University Press, 1999); Margaret Ruth Miles, *Image as Insight: Visual Understanding in Western Christianity and Secular Culture* (Boston: Beacon Press, 1985).

2. The story of the iconoclastic challenge to Eastern Byzantium is a fascinating one. For a theologian, it is crucial knowledge. The reader might be interested in this story told expertly in the following: Moshe Barasch, *Icon Studies in the History of an Idea* (New York: New York University Press, 1992); Louis Bréhier, *La Querelle Des Images (VIIIe-IXe Siècles)* (New York: B. Franklin, 1969); Ambrosios Giakalis, *Images of the Divine: The Theology of Icons at the Seventh Ecumenical Council,* Studies in the History of Christian Thought (Leiden/New York: E. J. Brill, 1994); André Grabar, *L'Iconoclasme Byzantin le Dossier Archéologique* (Paris: Flammarion, 1984); Jaroslav Jan Pelikan, *Imago Dei: The Byzantine Apologia for Icons* (Washington, D.C. [Princeton, N.J.]: National Gallery of Art Princeton University Press, 1990); Christoph von Schönborn, *God's Human Face: The Christ-Icon* (San Francisco: Ignatius Press, 1994).

3. Peter Brown, "Images as Substitute for Writing," in *East and West Modes of Communication: Proceedings of the First Plenary Conference at Merida,* vol. v. 5, edited by Euangelos K. Chrysos and I. N. Wood, Transformation of the Roman World (Leiden/Boston: Brill, 1999) 15ff., as quoted in Herbert L. Kessler, *Spiritual Seeing: Picturing God's Invisibility in Medieval Art,* The Middle Ages Series (Philadelphia: University of Pennsylvania Press, 2000) 104.

4. As quoted in Alain Besançon, *The Forbidden Image: An Intellectual History of Iconoclasm* (Chicago: University of Chicago Press, 2000) 149.

5. This phrase is well known. David Freedberg offers a good analysis of its implications for Christian art. David Freedberg, *The Power of Images Studies in the History and Theory of Response* (Chicago: University of Chicago Press, 1989) 162.

6. This belief has a philosophical basis in the faculty psychology of Aristotle and the development of the notion of the will by St. Augustine. The principle here is to get the will out of its "inertia" and moving so it can decisively act. Emotions do this more effectively than intellectual abstractions. Once the will begins to move then intellectual notions can guide the will in making true changes in a lifestyle. In other words, emotions move one, in Cardinal Newman's terms, from "intellectual assent" to "real assent." As Newman put it: "Many a man will live and die upon a dogma; no man will be a martyr to a conclusion." John Henry Cardinal Newman, *An Essay in Aid of a Grammar of Assent,* with an introduction by Nicholas Lash (Notre Dame: University of Notre Dame Press, 1979) 89. Nonetheless, this assertion by Pope Gregory was also a pastoral observation. Margaret Miles offers a good summary of medieval belief in the power of art to engage the emotions and, thus, the will. Margaret Ruth Miles, *Image as Insight: Visual Understanding in Western Christianity and Secular Culture,* 66ff.

7. Besançon, op. cit., 150.

8. I am referring to the "aesthetic nominalism" of an earlier chapter. From the medieval, religious art developed in the direction of greater and greater subjectivism. The

end result was the absolute subjectivity of the artist that is one symptom of an "aesthetic nominalism."

9. I do not intend to give a lengthy introduction to the theological system of Pseudo-Dionysius. Such an undertaking requires an entire book in itself! Although I plan to elaborate a bit more on Pseudo-Dionysius, I would refer the reader to these various works. For a readable collection of Dionysius' works, I recommend Pseudo-Dionysius, Colm Luibhéid, and Paul Rorem, *Pseudo-Dionysius, the Complete Works,* translated by Colm Luibhéid (New York: Paulist Press, 1987). For an insightful exposition on his system, the following are worth exploring. Andrew Louth, *Denys, the Areopagite* (Wilton, Conn.: Morehouse, 1989); Fran O'Rourke, *Pseudo-Dionysius and the Metaphysics of Aquinas,* Studien und Texte Zur Geistesgeschichte Des Mittelalters (Leiden/New York: E. J. Brill, 1992); René Roques, *L'Univers Dionysien Structure Hiérarchique Du Monde Selon le Pseudo-Denys,* Théologie ([Paris]: Aubier, 1954); Paul Rorem, *Pseudo-Dionysius: A Commentary on the Texts and an Introduction to Their Influence* (New York: Oxford University Press, 1993).

10. An interesting parallel lies in the theological aesthetics of Jonathan Edwards, a Puritan theologian. Impressed by Locke's *Essay Concerning Human Understanding,* Perry Miller describes the religious experience of Edwards, an experience strikingly similar to the medieval aesthetic experience: "The boy had walked in his father's pasture, looking upon the sky and clouds until 'the appearance of every thing was altered' and 'there seemed to be, as it were, a calm, sweet, cast, or appearance of divine glory, in almost every thing'; he used to sit and view the moon, 'singing forth, with a low voice, my contemplations of the Creator.' His mind became 'greatly fixed on divine things; almost perpetually in the contemplation of them,' until his inability to express what he felt became a torturing clog and a burden: 'The inward ardour of my soul, seemed to be hindered and pent up, and could not freely flame out as it would.' Then he read Locke, and the divine strategy was revealed to him. God's way, Locke made clear, is indirection, which is the only way, because speaking the unspeakable is impossible; God works through the concrete and the specific, and the mind (Edwards would add the regenerate mind) must know enough 'to stop when it is at the utmost extent of its tether.'" The striking difference between the medievals and Edwards was that Edwards proposed to elevate "regenerate experience" to a higher spiritual plane by the expressiveness of words rather than the expressiveness of visual art. Nonetheless, Edwards' theological aesthetics is witness to the perennial issues involved in theological aesthetics. Perry Miller, *Jonathan Edwards* (Amherst, Mich.: University of Massachusetts Press, 1981) 24.

11. Bernard of Clairvaux wrote this as part of a larger *Apologia* protesting the "backsliding" of Benedictine monasteries in the observance of the Rule of St. Benedict. Although the protest was aimed at the lavish art being displayed then at many Benedictine monasteries, such as the one at Suger's St-Denis, the protest was less an iconoclastic critique than a call to Benedictine reform. Bernard was no iconoclast. The insightful and expressive way Bernard describes the subjects of much medieval art shows exquisite sensitivity to the aesthetics he found objectionable. Indeed, the great art historian, Erwin Panofsky, remarked that art historians ought well to consider this paragraph from the *Apologia* as a model for their writing. Bernard (of Clairvaux), *Apologia Ad Guillelmum Abbatrem,* in *Sancti Bernardi Opera,* edited by Jean Leclercq and H. M. Rochais (Rome, 1957–77), XI, 29, as provided as an appendix in Conrad Rudolph and Bernard, *The "Things of Greater Importance": Bernard of Clairvaux's Apologia and the Medieval Attitude Toward Art* (Philadelphia: University of Pennsylvania Press, 1990).

12. Panofsky attributes this shift to a more animated lifelike rendition of subjects to the Aristotelian ascendance in Scholasticism. Aristotle made the "soul" or form inextricable from its material "body" unlike Platonism which saw the "soul" or form abstracted from its material "body." See, Erwin Panofsky, *Gothic Architecture and Scholasticism* (New York: Meridian Books, 1957) 6ff.

13. Thus, in the Renaissance, artists like Raphael would be called "divine artist" because in their skill at creating a spiritual work of art, they modeled almost perfectly the divine skill of the Creator.

14. Otto Georg von Simson, *The Gothic Cathedral Origins of Gothic Architecture and the Medieval Concept of Order,* Bollingen Series (New York: Pantheon Books, 1962) 104.

15. In this context, Gothic can be seen as the expression of French medieval art.

16. John F. Benton, "Introduction: Suger's Life and Personality," in *Abbot Suger and Saint-Denis: A Symposium,* edited by Paula Lieber Gerson (New York: Metropolitan Museum of Art, 1986) 3ff.

17. *De Administratione,* XXXIV, 5, as given in Suger and Erwin Panofsky, *Abbot Suger on the Abbey Church of St.-Denis and Its Art Treasures,* edited by Erwin Panofsky (Princeton, N.J.: Princeton University Press, 1948) 40–80.

18. A fine account of this theological tradition can be found in Carol Harrison, *Beauty and Revelation in the Thought of Saint Augustine,* Oxford Theological Monographs (Oxford [England]/New York: Clarendon Press/Oxford University Press, 1992); David C. Lindberg, *Theories of Vision from al-Kindi to Kepler* (Chicago: University of Chicago Press, 1976); Arthur Zajonc, *Catching the Light the Entwined History of Light and Mind* (New York: Bantam Books, 1993).

19. Harrison, op. cit., 116–17.

20. *De Genesi Ad Litteram,* 12.26 as quoted in Kessler, op. cit., 118.

21. An excellent exposition of Augustine's notion of "intellectual vision" can be found in Margaret Miles, "Vision: The Eye of Body and the Eye of the Mind in St. Augustine's *De Trinitate* and the *Confessions," Journal of Religion* 163, no. 2 (April 1983) 125–42.

22. Augustine, *De Genesi ad Litteram,* 12.23 as quoted in Kessler, op. cit., 120.

23 Hans Urs von Balthasar interprets Pseudo-Dionysius differently than most scholars. He sees his system as less a syncretic borrowing of Neoplatonism than a highly original, authentic Christian theology. Although, this view is not mainstream it is highly respected. Indeed, there is, I think, no better essay on Dionysius' thought than the essay von Balthasar wrote for volume two of his theological aesthetics, *The Glory of the Lord.* I highly recommend this essay to the reader. See Hans Urs von Balthasar and John Kenneth Riches, "Dionysius," in *Studies in Theological Style: Clerical Styles,* vol. 2 of *The Glory of the Lord,* edited by John Kenneth Riches, translated by John Kenneth Riches (San Francisco/New York: Ignatius Press/Crossroad, 1984).

24. The association of light with God comes directly from the prologue to John's Gospel. In the prologue, the divine Logos is presented as the Light that shines in the darkness. There is as well an indirect association of Light with God through Platonic thought. Plato used the metaphor of cave dwellers rising out of the darkness of their ignorance to the liberating full sunlight of the Good. Neoplatonists took Plato's metaphor and gave it concreteness in a metaphysical system in which light is a transcendental reality in which every creature partakes in some way. Light is also that which illumines our intellect in the understanding of the world around us.

25. Abbot Suger, *De Administratione,* XXXIII as provided in Suger and Panofsky, op. cit., 63–65.

26. Suger, *De Administratione,* XXXVII as provided in Suger and Panofsky, op. cit., 48–49.

"The Dog, the Cat, and the Mouse"

CHAPTER FIVE

The Human Aspect of Atonement

There is an artistic equivalent to views that see ignorance as innocence. I am referring to popular religious art. This is the art one finds on bedroom dressers and living room walls. It is the art found on holy cards and street vendor carts. It is the religious art of simple folk. From the point of view of a dynamic innocence, however, such art often contains a powerful theological dimension. In this chapter, I take a look at religious art that is often considered *kitsch,* that is, in bad taste. Such art is often mass produced and sold not at galleries but in the streets or in the small shops found at many churches. An example of such art is one found in many holy cards. A special holy card for many people of Latin America and the United States is that of the famous mulatto saint from Peru, St. Martin de Porres.

St. Martin de Porres, dressed in his Dominican habit, oversees a cat, a dog, and a mouse drinking from the same bowl of soup. To the cynical or the arrogant aesthete, this image of St. Martin represents a static innocence, the art of those ignorant of refined and sublime works. If the view of the cynic is true, then millions of folks have terribly bad taste, for this image of St. Martin de Porres is, perhaps, the most popular religious image in the Americas second only to that of Our Lady of Guadalupe. The image of St. Martin de Porres may seem *kitsch* to the aesthetic sophisticate, but even they cannot deny the great spiritual power of the image. Nor can they explain it.

The reason, I will suggest, is that the *aesthete* fails to note the difference between sophistication and cultivation, between a static innocence and a dynamic one. Sophistication aims at overcoming a static innocence. As such, it sets itself against the theological dimension in art. That dimension, as I have been arguing, is about a wounded innocence, about a religious insight into the need and way of salvation. Art is about experience: not in order to lose one's innocence but in order to gain it. Thus, sophistication works against the theological roots of art and, if unchecked, degenerates into anti-art, as Duchamp's *Fountain* so clearly represents.

Cultivation, on the other hand, is sophistication gained in the process of a dynamic innocence. Cultivation is not inimical to innocence but depends on it for its sophistication. As such, cultivation and culture are related but not identical.[1] Cultivation is not the product of a culture but the work of a community. The cultivated or "cultured" are folks who grasp the theological dimension of art by virtue of the insights they have gained in the communal interpretation of their present as their past is contrasted with their future. The "cultured" are interpreters of their lived realities as it is lived in the garden of good and evil. For this reason, the "cultured" seek not to interpret the evil in their lives. Evil needs no interpretation. It is self-evident. What needs to be explained is the true, the good, and the beautiful. For that is not only the very stuff of life but also life's motivation. One lives for a world of truth, and goodness, and beauty. A world without these is not worth living for.

The "cultured," then, draw on all their accumulated wisdom and experience to interpret that which offers life. The "cultured," in other words, know of their need of salvation and seek to interpret the way to that salvation. In this endeavor, no interpretation is more powerful than that of the beautiful. The beautiful, in a profound and theological sense, is an interpretation of the way of salvation. A work of art can subvert evil in its very roots by creating a vision of humanity that is so healing, so hopeful, so beautiful that it would not have been possible if the evil had not taken place. Thus evil itself becomes the source of a beauty that becomes a power for a life of truth, goodness, and the beautiful. Evil, having given root to life, fades away like a mist before the morning sun. Thus, Art, in its theological dimension, can be said to participate in the mystery of the Atonement. As such, Art reveals the *human* aspect of the Atonement. Perhaps no other art is as revealing of this aspect as popular religious art.

The Anthropomorphites and Popular Religious Art

David Morgan, in his highly acclaimed book *Visual Piety,* sees two opposed views to the relationship between art and religion. As he put it, "either art is the handmaiden of religion, or else the artist is an autonomous agent working out of his or her own inspiration, which may or may not parallel the specific concerns of religion."[2] Popular religious art, on the other hand, plays havoc with such oppositions. Popular religious art tends to blur the line between the individual artist and the community of religious fervor. Those who buy the holy card and are inspired by its image do not ask who is responsible for it. There is a profound sense in which the image is thought to emerge out of the very soul of the community's devotion. Indeed, the artist responsible for the holy card image of St. Martin de Porres could be said to be the community itself.

Popular religious art, in opposing such dualism, finds a difficult place not only in the art world of today but also in theology. The problem, let me suggest, can be traced by a view of aesthetics that has been tremendously influential. I am speaking of the aesthetics articulated by Immanuel Kant, the great Enlightenment philosopher. Kant saw the experience of true beauty as one of "disinterestedness." In other words, true aesthetic experience is "disinterested." Popular religious art, on the other hand, is anything but disinterested. Popular religious art engages in a very personal way the emotions of the beholder.

As such, popular religious art raises the issue of the nature of the spirituality of art. Kant's "aesthetic disinterestedness," for example, parallels what theologians call an "apophatic" spirituality. "Apophatic" derives from two Greek words. "Apo" means "to remove or take away," and "phatic" refers to "feelings, passion." In other words, "apophatic" spirituality tries to detach itself from any kind of feelings or passion in order to make space for the possibility of the presence of God. In contrast, popular religious art, in the language of spirituality, is "kataphatic," i.e., "filled with passion." Kant's aesthetics of "disinterestedness" draws a line between the passionate and the contemplative. It tempts us to see another set of dualisms, the "apophatic" versus the "kataphatic," the mystical versus the everyday, the religious elite versus the religious ordinary.[3]

This temptation is dangerous to a theology of art. For the apple of this temptation contains the worm of iconoclasm. The line between "apophatic" and iconoclasm is a fine one and has caused theological debate before. Under Kant's influence this line gets blurred, or, worse, ceases to exist altogether, and the spirituality of art seen under the light of "aesthetic disinterestedness" is seen more and more as an "apophatic" spirituality that becomes an iconoclasm. The remedy for this lies in recognizing the continuity between passionate ("kataphatic") and contemplative ("apophatic") spirituality. This was the issue emerging out of the deserts of Egypt in the fourth century over the monk's use of popular religious art.

The issue concerned the use of images in prayer. At stake lay an understanding of what it means to be an "image of God" within the garden of good and evil. Christianity had not yet won a total victory over the pagan religions of Egypt. Indeed, many of the monks who had retreated into the desert had not made much of a distinction between their old pagan religion and the new Christian religion. Part of the challenge of the leaders and masters of the community of desert monks was the education and formation of these recent converts to Christianity on the content and nature of Christian beliefs.[4] Many of these new monks had interpreted the Christian belief that the human creature was made in the image of God literally, i.e., literally in a pagan "reverse" sort of way. For these once-pagan monks reasoned that since we had arms and legs and we were made in the image of God, then God must also have arms and legs! This belief was known as the Anthropomorphite heresy and it ran rampant in Egypt of the fourth century. The anthropomorphite monks of the desert kept their old traditions alive by having statues or paintings of "God" by which they entered into prayer. Not only was such practice a continuity with their pagan past, it was also an ancient example of popular religious art.

The Desert Fathers addressed the anthropomorphite tendencies of their monks through their teaching on imageless prayer. Perhaps the best articulation of such prayer is by a monk who lived in the twentieth century, Thomas Merton. As he put it: "One has begun to know the meaning of contemplation when he intuitively and spontaneously seeks the dark and unknown path of aridity in preference to every other way. The contemplative . . . accepts the love of God on faith, in defiance of all apparent evidence. This is the necessary condition, for that mystical experience of the reality of God's presence and of his love for us. Only when we are able to 'let go' of everything within us, all desire to see, to know, to taste and to experience that presence with the overwhelming conviction and reality that revolutionize our entire inner life."[5] Imageless prayer, however, had an ambiguity built in. In its "apophatic" letting-go approach, it gives the impression of an iconoclasm. John Cassian describes a famous "conference" in which the ambiguous iconoclastic nature of imageless prayer was addressed by a profound teacher, Abbot Isaac. It involved a simple monk named Serapion.

Serapion most probably was one of those recent converts from Egyptian paganism. He had a statue or image of "God" which he used for his prayers and meditation. Serapion, most likely, was a practical if not a self-conscious Anthropomorphite. In this Serapion most probably represented many of the desert monks. While Serapion meditated on his image of "God," Emperor Theophilus had started purging his diocese of Egyptian idols and temples.[6] It did not take long for Theophilus' fervor against images to catch up with simple Serapion's use of images. Theophilus was aware of the Anthropomorphite tendencies among the desert monks. Thus, Theophilus sent a letter to be read among the desert monks denouncing the Anthropomorphite heresy and declaring in the most explicit terms that God was an "invisible" God and could not be portrayed in an image.

Serapion was crushed. He exclaimed, "Woe is me, wretch that I am! They have taken my God from me, and I have no one to lay hold of, nor do I know whom I should adore or address."[7] The monks brought Serapion's grief to the attention of Abbot Isaac. Serapion's grief, after all, was the grief of many other monks who suddenly found themselves at the brink of an insidious iconoclasm. Abbot Isaac, to his credit, defended Serapion's grief even while acknowledging his Anthropomorphite error. Abbot Isaac, then, began to explain to the monks the nature of imageless prayer. Abbot Isaac explained to them that the aim of imageless prayer was to "address God with purity and integrity of heart" in order "to possess the image of future blessedness in this body and as it were to begin to taste the pledge of that heavenly way of life and glory in this vessel."[8]

And what is this blessedness-in-body? It is Jesus "seen by the soul's inward gaze—either as still humble and in the flesh or glorified and coming in the glory of his majesty."[9] In other words, the aim of imageless prayer is an image! Or, rather, one should say a vision. Such vision, however, is not achieved without passion. Indeed, as Cassian tells us, "they alone see his Godhead with purest eyes who, mounting from humble and earthly tasks and thoughts, go off with him to the lofty mountain of the desert, which free from the uproar of every earthly thought and disturbance, removed from every taint of vice, and exalted with the purest faith and soaring virtue, reveals the glory of his face and the image of his brightness to those who deserve to look upon him with the clean gaze of the soul."[10]

This analogy of religious aesthetic experience to the Transfiguration sounds strange to ears conditioned by understanding of aesthetics formulated by Kant. It speaks of a tremendous spiritual passion, a struggle of heroic proportions, to achieve a certain "purity" or innocence in order to "see." There is a profound aesthetic dimension in the Transfiguration analogy of Abbot Isaac. It is the image of following our Lord up a long climb to the top of a mountain where a new kind of seeing takes place. Following Christ up a long and difficult climb signifies a process of sanctification. It is a process towards that blessedness that will allow us a marvelous vision. It is, indeed, a climb from the woundedness of the world into an innocence of vision. It is the attaining of a wounded innocence.

The Transfiguration analogy given to us by Abbot Isaac underscores the continuity between passion and contemplation, between passionate spirituality and contemplative spirituality, between the "kataphatic" and the "apophatic."[11] As such, it also suggests an answer to the Anthropomorphite heresy that avoids iconoclasm. The continuity between passion and contemplation is a wounded innocence. Achieving such innocence involves the following of Christ up a spiritual Mount Tabor. The Anthropomorphite heresy centered on what it meant for the human to be created in the image of God. What kind of image is the human if the human is an image of God? The anthropomorphites answered it by saying: God looks like us! The iconoclastic answer was given by Bishop Theophilus. No image does justice to God so all images of God must be banished. In his unbridled iconoclasm, Bishop Theophilus failed to account for an image that does justice to God. What kind of image does justice to the image of God? It is the image of Christ! Christ, as St. Paul says, is the image of the invisible God. In Christ, we see what it means to be an image of God. As such, we become the image of Christ not in trying to "look" like Christ but in following Christ. In the imitation of Christ, we become "conformed" to Christ's image. And to become one with Christ's image is also to become one with the image of God.

By suggesting the following of Christ up Mount Tabor in order to understand what it means to be an image of God, Isaac uncovers the aesthetic dimension of a long and ancient tradition known as the *imitatio Christi*. For the monk, this means the path of imageless prayer. This path is not an iconoclasm for its aim is an image. Although Abbot Isaac does not elaborate, he mentions that for those of us who are not monks, there is another path to the marvelous vision promised in imageless prayer. It is, I think, the path of popular religious art.

Popular Religious Art

Though few theologies today wrestle with the issues of popular religious art, one group of theologians have engaged this struggle in a significant way. I am speaking of the Academy of Catholic Hispanic

Theologians in the United States (better known as ACHTUS). This small group of theologians against great odds, few resources, and the skepticism of an entrenched theological establishment, have engaged the issue of popular religion and its images. The issue is important to Hispanic theology for its context is an ecclesial tradition that has its roots in the sixteenth-century conquest of America. In that conquest, indigenous and European religious worldviews merged in a powerful, authentically American Christianity expressed in an amazing variety of aesthetic forms. Divine images, paintings, sculptures, plays, processions, and music make up the bulk of Latin American and Hispanic popular religion. Hispanic theologians studying these images (at the amazement of the established theological institutions) have uncovered profound religious insights that are deeply and powerfully spiritual and liberating.[12]

Hispanic theology has, like Abbot Isaac, struggled with the implications of the *imago Dei*. In the case of the Americas, the issue concerned a theological iconoclasm the likes of which the dear abbot could not have imagined. The unequal and violent encounter of Europe with America raised a tremendous theological issue. European Christianity believed all peoples in the world had descended from the three sons of Noah. Each of the three sons, Shem, Ham, and Japheth, represented respectively the nations of Europe, Africa, and Asia. All human ethnicity belonged to one of these three ethnic groups. Since this ethnic grouping was derived from Sacred Scripture, its classification of peoples was tantamount to sacred revelation. Imagine, then, the theological conundrum of finding a new people in the Americas!

For those who wished to exploit the labor and wealth of the New World, appeal to this sacred configuration was a convenient way to justify a merciless exploitation. Such folk argued that the Amerindian was a *homunculus,* a subhuman. Theologians scrambled against such beliefs. At stake was building a new Christianity in the New World. If the Amerindians were *homunculi,* then they were not created in the image of God and could not be baptized. Fortunately, few theologians believed this incredible thesis and saw it for what it was. Theologians, however, had their work cut out for them. The mark of being in the image of God was rationality. The Amerindian was seen as intuitive rather than rational. The source of this belief was the incredible cultural difference between indigenous America and Iberian Europe. The languages, customs, and religious beliefs of the American Indian seemed irrational and superstitious to a Europe just emerging out of the Middle Ages.[13] Theologians, such as Bartolomé de las Casas, were able to successfully defend the humanity of the Amerindian. They were not able, however, to convince the hard of heart. To this day, there still remains suspicion by many of the fullness of the humanity of the American Indian and their descendants, the *mestizos,* or mixed-race children of European and Indian parents, that make up the majority of Hispanics and Latin Americans today.

Out of this great theological debate emerged a new Christianity of the Americas. Its marks were a concern for beauty and for justice. Because of the great cultural and language differences, Christian doctrine was taught to the Indians by aesthetic means. Music, drama, paintings, statues, and images not only were able to communicate far better than texts or words but they also gave witness to the humanity of the Indian. No animal plays an instrument or takes up oils and creates a painting. More important, no animal can appreciate beauty the way a human does. In any case, American Christianity emerged with a tradition of a love for art and beauty rather than a schoolish love of books and words. The great prejudice against the indigenous also gave another mark to this emerging Christianity, a passion for justice. The question of being made in the image of God became less and less an academic exercise and more and more a political and legal struggle.

To this day, the Latin Church of the Americas struggles with prejudice against her people.[14] Indeed, many of America's faithful are seen if not as subhuman, then as naïve children who must be treated with condescension and a firm hand. It is a continuing struggle to define what it means to be in the image of God. The doctrine of the image of God has become for America's faithful a question of justice. As such, it has become a struggle of innocence. Such innocence is not one to defend after false accusations nor is it one to be lost because of a dangerous naïveté. Rather, the struggle of innocence in the Americas is one to be achieved in the garden of good and evil. It is an innocence to subvert the evil that would destroy the dignity of our humanity. It is a wounded innocence that subverts evil at its very roots. Indeed, it is the mark of true justice.

These two marks, beauty and justice, give American Christianity a distinctive ecclesial flavor within the larger Roman Catholic tradition. Inextricably mixed with the official rituals of the Roman Catholic Church are the colors, sounds, and images of Hispanic and Latin American popular religious art. Though some see such art as opposed to the official liturgies and doctrines of the Church, popular religious art, as the work of the theologians of ACHTUS shows, actually uncovers the depth and profundity of the larger Roman Catholic tradition. Such art was able to navigate the charge that Hispanics were less than the image of God by the artistic presentation of beauty in harmony with justice. A new challenge, however, emerged in the late twentieth century. A new kind of iconoclasm began to rise which threatened the harmony of beauty and justice that American Christianity had exquisitely woven.

The end of the twentieth century saw a righteous impatience with the miserable conditions of the poor of Latin America. Liberation theology was the first of a series of contemporary theologies to address this scandalous situation. Perhaps one of liberation theology's greatest gifts to the Church is its transformation of the *imitatio Christi* towards a concern for justice. One enters into the mystery of suffering with our Lord in order to discover and enter the process of salvation. This process, however, is concrete as well as spiritual and calls for a kind of following that is also concrete. This concrete following of Christ in order to enter the process of salvation is called *praxis*. *Praxis* means following Christ towards a self-conscious attempt to discover and dismantle social systems that dehumanize and oppress the poor. In this sense, the *imitatio Christi* becomes in liberation theology what I have called a religious insight.

Liberation theology's adoption of the *imitatio Christi* anthropology, however, often put it at odds with popular religion and its art. Liberation theology has had an ambivalent attitude to popular religion and its images and rituals. The episcopal conference that took place in Medellín, for example, begins its document on "pastoral popular" speaking of popular religion as a "deformed" kind of religiosity.

> Among the great masses of the baptized in Latin America, the conditions of faith, Christian beliefs and practices vary widely, not only from country to country but even from one region to another within the same country, and among different social classes. There are semi-pagan ethnic groups, peasant masses which are still deeply religious and marginal masses, which have religious sentiments, but which cannot be labeled as practicing.[15]

On the other hand, there is a kind of positive recognition given to popular religion by the bishops. They acknowledge that popular religion can contain authentic Christian elements. Thus, religious expressions of the poor can contain "stammerings of an authentic religious sense."[16]

Liberation theology reflects the ambivalent attitude articulated by the bishops of Medellín but not in the same proportion. Most liberation theologians take a more positive view than the bishops at Medellín.

Gustavo Gutiérrez, for example, sees in popular religion "the presence of an immense liberating potential."[17] Gutiérrez here speaks for the majority of liberation theologians. Nonetheless, there exists a sizeable group that sees popular religion in a negative light. Enrique Dussel, for example, sees popular religion as a "passing, moribund phenomenon." Perhaps Diego Irarrazaval is the most outspoken of this negative view. As he puts it,

> They are practices that separate Christians from the revolutionary attempt to destroy the capitalist roots of domination. Instead of taking history in their own hands, they trust that the solidarity of the oppressed will forge a linking solidarity with other knowing believers. Instead of taking history into their own hands, they trust in miracles. Instead of struggling with and for all, they want to receive something with and for a few. In the light of these facts, religious practice appears to separate the people from a true revolutionary praxis.[18]

Thus, with one group of liberation theologians, popular religious art was often seen as an obstacle to following Christ in the process of salvation.

Under the influence of this group a kind of iconoclasm began to show its face. Some priests began to strip their churches of all statues leaving only a single crucifix as an object of devotion.[19] Thus, another iconoclastic movement became active in certain groups of liberation theology-minded communities. The aesthetic promise of the *imitatio Christi* tradition now became a paradox under the notion of *praxis*. Instead of defending the dignity of the human person as an image of God, it now became the source of yet another iconoclasm.

Roberto Goizueta, in his *Caminemos con Jesús,* addressed this implicit iconoclasm in liberation theology by taking a new look at the meaning of *praxis*.[20] Goizueta pointed out that certain understandings of *praxis* in liberation theology lead to a highly individualistic sense of following. Goizueta further tells us that when the imitation of Christ is read in an individualistic sense, it pits justice against beauty. He points to the fact that the imitation of Christ has two directions. Yes, we follow Christ, but Christ also accompanies us in our following. This double dynamism in imitation, "following" and "accompanying," reveals an intersubjective, communal dimension in the imitation of Christ. In other words, the imitation of Christ can be interpreted in a highly individualistic sense or in a highly communal sense. The ambivalence in liberation theology to popular religion lies in its failing to make clear the double dynamism in a Christian understanding of *praxis*.

What Goizueta makes clear is that the *imitatio Christi* tradition uncovers the communal dimension of image. The communal dimension of image reveals a dynamic element that is hidden from an understanding of image as simply a copy of an original. The communal dimension of image opens up an aesthetic understanding of image that includes the moral and ethical dimensions inherent in a theological aesthetics. Goizueta's brilliant analysis on the relationship between justice and beauty does much to help tease out the underlying roots of the implicit iconoclasm in liberation theology. Interpreting the imitation of Christ in a communal sense reveals that justice and beauty nourish and sustain each other. Goizueta's work reveals an important insight. Iconoclasm has as its roots the loss of the communal dimension of image.

Goizueta, however, leaves unclear the nature of divine accompaniment. Does Jesus merely accompany us in our suffering? Or is salvation a present reality in the accompaniment and following of Christ? In other words, does imitating Christ take us simply onto the Cross? Or does it take us as well into the Resurrection? If justice and beauty are reconciled in the following and accompanying of Christ, then *imitatio Christi* does not simply refer to our need of salvation but also to the way of salvation. If Beauty can not save, then it has no relationship to Justice. Thus, imitating Christ means following Christ not only onto the Cross but also into his Resurrection.

What does it mean to follow Christ onto the Cross and into his Resurrection? Let me suggest the poignant image of the risen Christ inviting his apostles to touch his wounds as the aesthetic dimension of the *imitatio Christi*. The imitation of Christ is not only following Christ onto the Cross or, even, Jesus accompanying us in our wounds. It is, in a crucial sense, accepting the invitation of the risen Jesus to touch his wounds. Here lies the aesthetic element missing in many accounts of the *imitatio Christi*. The imitation of Christ consists not only in following and accompanying but also in touching and seeing.

Here lies the profundity of the invitation offered to the doubting Thomas. The invitation to touch his wounds urges Thomas to choose innocence over cynicism, to choose wonder over security. Thomas followed Jesus up to the cross. Now Thomas must follow Jesus into his resurrection by the aesthetic act of touching. The aesthetic dimension of the imitation of Christ culminates in the invitation to follow Jesus into a new innocence by touching the wounds of the risen, wounded, and innocent Christ. Indeed, the religious insight of the imitation of Christ lies less in the heroic bearing of wounds than participating in a wounded innocence. It is in this wounded innocence that Justice and Beauty find their unity. It is in this wounded innocence where the human creature conforms to the image of Christ that, in turn, allows us to see ourselves as an image of God.

Here, I believe, lies the spiritual power in the best of popular religious art. Popular religious art, at its best, offers the beholder a religious insight into salvation by inviting one, in an artistic sense, to touch the wounds of the risen Christ. In doing so, something more than following and accompaniment, compassion, and sympathy takes place. There is an insight into evil itself that subverts it at its very roots for it offers a vision of humanity that is more beautiful than if the evil had not taken place. Popular religious art, at its best, interprets humanity to the human from within the garden of good and evil. In doing so, it offers a new innocence of vision that would not have been possible had there been no struggle for justice. For a marvelous example of this dimension of popular religious art, let us return to the popular image of the mulatto saint of Peru, St. Martin de Porres.

St. Martin de Porres

In the seventeenth century, a great mystery took place in Lima, Peru. The good people of Lima had the nerve to propose as saint a local known as Martin de Porres. Even worse, this local was the illegitimate child of Ana Velasquez, a freed African slave, and Don Juan de Porres, a Spanish gentleman. Martin de Porres, in other words, was of mixed-race, a mulatto whose father had not had the decency to make him legitimate by marrying his mother. This was not unusual. Spanish gentlemen did not marry former African slaves.

To add to absurdity, this proposal came at a time when the Church in Europe was shaken by Reformation attacks on the abuse of the veneration of saints. Rome was in no mood to consider any new saints. Rome was even less in the mood to consider a saint from the Americas. The Americas, after all, were a mission field. The Christians there did not have the depth of faith that the more established Christians of Europe had. More important, the Christians of the Americas were influenced by indigenous religions and one could not be sure if they were really Christian. In the case of this mulatto, it was quite likely that he had Moorish, that is, Islamic leanings. To add insult to injury, this potential Muslim was not even legitimate.

How could the Church even consider such a candidate as a saint? What made the people of Lima think they even had a chance of getting their local Martin de Porres considered for sainthood? Herein lies the mystery. If the people of Lima had wanted the honor of having a local named a saint of the Church, they should have proposed someone of European parents that had a long Catholic history or waited until things cooled down in Europe. Yet they did neither of these. There was something special about Martin de Porres, and the people of Lima knew it.

According to the census of 1613, Lima had an estimated 9,600 Spanish families, 2,000 indigenous, 10,400 of African descent, slave and free, and approximately 1,000 of mixed-race. As such, it resembled a prototype of a modern urban city with its various ethnic groupings. The social structure of Lima at the time consisted of the "Peninsulares" or Spanish-born aristocracy who held the highest positions of power and church office, the "Criollos" or native born of Spanish heritage who held the minor but powerful church and governmental posts, and the mestizos, biological and cultural hybrids of African, Indian, and Iberian blood, who were said to "have the vices of both races and the virtues of neither."

This last category determined St. Martin's social place in Lima of the sixteenth century. As such St. Martin lived at the boundaries of many social groups. St. Martin would always be at the periphery of the Iberians, Indians, and Africans of Lima. Characteristically enough, St. Martin decided to join the Dominicans not as a regular lay brother which would have placed him inside the boundary of the religious order but as a "donado" or Tertiary, which literally placed him at the boundaries of the convent, taking care of the sick and of the domestic duties of the order.

As a Dominican, Martín flowered and we have many stories of his life in the convent.[21] He would awake every day ringing the dawn bell at 4 A.M. He visited sick in priory. He was in charge of the linens, collecting, washing, and distributing them. After the noon meal, he distributed at the infirmary door food and necessities to the poor white, Indian, African, and mestizo. Then he would go out into the city of Lima begging for alms.

For being a mere Tertiary, St. Martín was, oddly enough, visited by men of high rank in Church and state, such as, Juan de Figueroa, "regidor" of Lima and "familiar" at the Court of Inquisition. Others included the Count of Chinchon, the viceroy of Peru, and Feliciano de la Vega who later became archbishop of Mexico. Part of the reason for these visits were the marvelous stories going around Lima of St. Martín's strange powers. Fray Porres, it was told, could walk through walls to get into places that people were sick. He could multiply himself to meet the demands of charity. One time, five assistants were sent to different parts of the convent to find Fray Martín. Amazingly, all found him, serving the sick at five different places at the same time! St. Martín also answered secret calls of the sick, prepared meals for them, and also took care of sick Indians and African slaves. Once, when he was found out to lodge Africans and Indians in his cell and was reprimanded, he is said to have responded: "Linens can be washed with soap and water, but sin of uncharity only by repentance." Moreover, Martin used to travel to the neighborhood known as Limatambo where he visited ill or needy Africans and Indians and also instructed them in Christian faith. On his way to Limatambo he would plant herbs and fruit trees along roadways so that any traveling sick could refresh themselves without need of entering private land.

Perhaps his most cherished attribute, however, was his manner with all sorts of animals. The following story is told of him: "When he would enter the chicken house of the infirmary, the chickens would rush toward him and cuddle up next to him and would let him pick them up and pet them and delighted by his company would act as if they had been loved dearly by him. And when he entered the stables the mules and the other beasts would lovingly and docilely come to him with signs of love and affection toward him. The same occurred with dogs, cats, and other house animals who exhibited great commotion when they saw him and rushed to him giving signs of their great affection for him nudging or licking him."[22] St. Martín was not only loved by the people of Lima but also by its animals!

Being loved by animals, became, one of the major "proofs" given by the people of Lima for St. Martín's sanctity. This may strike us at odd but if we remember that one of the hotly debated theological issues of the time was the nature of the human as the image of God, then the connection of sanctity with love of animals can be discerned. An animal, you see, was an "irrational" brute. Animals were not made in the image of God. The mark of that image was rationality. Thus, only human beings and angels could be said to possess reason. Because animals were "irrational," it was acceptable to treat them anyway you want. Often, they were cruelly, sadistically mistreated. It didn't take much of a leap of imagination for a citizen of Lima to see that others, the Indian, the African, and the mixed-race, were treated very much like the animals. Thus, when St. Martín began to heal animals who had been cruelly mistreated, the people in Lima saw here both a social and theological revolution. A typical story, for example, is told by Fray Fernando Aragones:

> And so all the friars, Indians and blacks, small and big, all took him as father, for relief and comfort through his works [of healing]; and this was not a miracle, for they were capable of reason; what seems out of all course and all that is natural is to see the animals who in not having any [reason], nor being capable of it, to recognize in said servant of God this charity.

The healing of animals and the feeding and clothing of the disenfranchised became in St. Martín de Porres a powerful theological statement. Being in the image of God amounts to more than mere rationality. The image of God involves being a community of love and care that knows no boundaries among creatures.[23]

San Martín died on November 3, 1639. It is said that he died at the moment the choir at his deathbed chanted the *homo factus est* ("and he became man") of the Credo. In 1660 Bishop Pedro de Villagómez, archbishop of Lima, began the process to canonize Fray Martín. Initially, sixty-five witnesses gave their testimony. Another one hundred and sixty-four witnesses were heard in the period 1678 to 1686. In 1763, Martín was beatified by Pope Gregory XVI. It was not, however, until May 6, 1962, that Blessed Martín was canonized by Pope John XXIII as a symbol of the spirit of Vatican II. By contrast, Santa Rosa de Lima, daughter of an aristocratic, white, Spanish family in Lima was canonized as saint by Pope Clement X in 1671. She had been baptized at the same baptismal font in the church of San Sebastian that San Martín had been baptized.[24] The only difference was that her baptism took place seven years later.

Yes, in St. Martín, a great mystery becomes manifest. It is the mystery of a great spiritual power that never lost hope that this child of the Americas would some day be recognized by his Church to be the holy man that he truly was. More important, the mystery of St. Martín is also the mystery of the Church in the Americas as it also yearns to be recognized for its faith and holiness by the wider Church. The holy card that is the subject of this chapter can probably be dated to the time before Blessed Martín became St. Martín. As such it is the embodiment of all the hopes and yearnings of a community whose faith has often been seen with suspicion. Theologically, it is an artistic rendering of the image of God. As such, it visually presents one of the most astounding stories told about St. Martín with profound religious insight.

Fray Fernando Aragones tells the following story:

> One of the Dominican friars in St. Martin's convent walked into a room near the kitchen to find a strange sight. At the feet of St. Martin were a dog and a cat eating peacefully from the same bowl of soup. The friar was about to call the rest of the monks in to witness this marvelous sight when a little mouse stuck his head out from a little hole in the wall. St. Martin without hesitation addressed the mouse as if he were an old friend. "Don't be afraid little one. If you're hungry come and eat with the others." The little mouse hesitated but then scampered to the bowl of soup from which the dog and the cat were eating. The friar who was watching all this take place tried to speak but no sound came out of his mouth. Here before his eyes, at the feet of the mulatto St. Martin, a dog, a cat, and a mouse were eating from the same bowl of soup, natural enemies eating peacefully side by side!

The best interpretation of this story can be found in the holy card image of this chapter. The key visual element is the white dove hovering above the bowl of soup and by the feet of St. Martín. The dove signifies a multitude of meanings. It signifies, for example, the spirit of peace. It interprets the dog, cat, and mouse all eating from the same bowl of soup as natural enemies now reconciled at the feet of the mulatto saint. The dove, however, also signifies the Holy Spirit who guided St. Martín's feet in the path of sanctity. Additionally, the dove signifies the boundary between rationality and irrationality, a boundary that can be crossed in the form of a community. As such, the dove also tells us that this image is also an image of the endtimes.[25]

Indeed, the image of St. Martín, in his habit as a Dominican friar, perhaps the order seen as the most "brainy" of all the orders, towering above the "irrational" creatures at his feet presents a vision of a marvelous community spoken about by Isaiah:

> "The wolf shall live with the lamb, the leopard shall lie down with the kid,
> the calf and the lion and the fatling together, and a little child shall
> lead them" (Isa 11:6).

That child is St. Martín who followed Christ in his mission of healing and forgiveness. St. Martín's imitation of Christ becomes in this image an actual representation of the image of God. As such, it reveals God's image as a deep religious insight. Although the human is the creature created in the image of God, the image of God involves a community, a community fully revealed in the endtimes. That is where the Holy Spirit is taking this world, transforming it under the guiding paths of her wings and the brilliant light of her wisdom.

Moreover, the dove also represents the *epiclesis* of the eucharistic ritual. As the Catholic Catechism tells us, "the *epiclesis* is at the heart of each sacramental celebration most especially of the Eucharist."[26] It is the coming down of the Holy Spirit to sanctify the bread and wine that will become for us the Body and Blood of Christ. As such, "the Holy Spirit's transforming power in the liturgy hastens the coming of the kingdom and the consummation of the mystery of salvation."[27] The *epiclesis* is also the Church's prayer for a community in union with the image of Christ. The image of St. Martín artistically rendered in this holy card is analogous to an *epiclesis*. The bowl of soup becomes an analogy to the eucharistic meal and the "irrational" animals the invited guests who contentedly and harmoniously form a community around it.

The eucharistic dimensions of the image refer once again to the image-of-God debate surrounding the people of the Americas. It may be hard for us to believe today, but the following questions were seriously asked in St. Martín's time: Were the people of the Americas worthy to share the eucharistic meal? Did they have the powers of reason to truly understand the mystery of the Eucharist?[28] In the eucharistic dimensions of our image of St. Martín, the question is answered with powerful "Yes." Indeed, the image strongly suggests that the true mystery of the eucharistic meal is inviting those felt to be unworthy to gather around the marvelous gift of our Lord's Body and Blood. The Eucharist is an invitation not for the purely just but for the repentant unjust, not for the simply innocent but for the wounded innocent. The mystery of the Eucharist revolves around transforming reconciliation rather than acknowledging justification. This is not yet, I believe, the religious insight of this image.

One can ask whether this image could have been made if it had not been for the great evil that took place in the conquest of the Americas? Let me suggest that it could not. As such, this image subverts this evil at its roots. It presents us with a new understanding of what it means to be in the image of God out of a great evil that used the doctrine of the image of God against God's own people. Indeed, if it had not been for this evil, the world would be poorer for not knowing the profundity of the doctrine of being created in the image of God. In this sense, the holy card image of St. Martin de Porres is an example of what I call (together with Josiah Royce) the human aspect of the Atonement.

As Goizueta demonstrated, the way of salvation revealed in the imitation of Christ is one of following and being accompanied by Christ, of compassion of Christ's wounds and sympathy of Christ and the Father for our wounds. The imitation of Christ culminates, as we have seen, in an encounter with the risen Jesus still carrying his wounds. In the image of St. Martin, the dog, the cat, and the mouse represent those wounds. Coupled visually to the innocence embodied by St. Martin who innocently healed dogs and cats as if they were human beings, one has the image of the risen, innocent, and wounded Christ. As such, it is another image of a wounded innocence.

The culmination of imitating Christ becomes visually accessible to us in the image of St. Martin feeding the dog, the cat, and the mouse. Such wounded innocence becomes a Latin American way to speak of the Atonement. The evil of this world becomes first transformed in the imitation of Christ into his Death and Resurrection and then, ultimately, into a wounded innocence that subverts evil at its very roots. A wounded innocence, in a sense, is the aesthetic application of that profound religious insight of the Suffering Servant: "[B]y his stripes we were healed" (Isa 53:5 NAB).

As such, the aesthetic interpretation of the imitation of Christ supports a *felix culpa* understanding of Atonement.[29] By *felix culpa,* I am referring to the *Exsultet* of the Easter Vigil, the liturgical tradition of singing *O felix culpa,* i.e., "O happy fault . . . which gained for us so great a Redeemer!" The theological aesthetic of *felix culpa* is patristic. If it were not for sin, we would not have known the wondrous redemptive grace of the Father in his Son through the Spirit. In other words, the world is better now because of sin than if sin had not entered the world. This may seem strange to our ears. But the *felix culpa* tradition is perhaps the most profound of Christian interpretations of evil.

The *felix culpa* tradition does not celebrate sin but, rather acknowledges the radical nature of evil. Rather than see evil as some "lesser" good, the *felix culpa* tradition sees evil as something to be engaged and overcome. It is overcome not by armed struggle or mindless activism. It is overcome by entering into its very roots and subverting it. In other words, sin is a *felix culpa* when, in overcoming it, the world is made better than if the sin had not been committed. The *felix culpa* tradition, indeed all atonement doctrines, rightly emphasize the unique role of Christ in atoning for the sins of the world. Nonetheless, there is a human aspect to the atonement that often gets overlooked.[30]

The crucified Christ and the risen Christ with wounds represent, in a sense, two aspects of the atonement. The crucified Christ emphasizes the unique role of Jesus in the Atonement. The risen Christ with wounds, on the other hand, suggests the participation of the human creature in the mystery of the Atonement. Indeed, the invitation by the risen Christ to touch his wounds can also be seen as an invitation to the human creature to participate in the *felix culpa* atonement made possible in Christ's death and resurrection. It is, in a sense, the traditional invitation to join Christ in the paschal mystery, to die and rise with him, by entering into the darkness of sin and subverting it at its root. Such subversion, I have suggested, is intrinsically aesthetic. If so, then there exists the possibility that one way to participate in the mystery of the Atonement is through Art itself.

The very invitation of the risen Jesus to touch his wounds, after all, is profoundly aesthetic. The holy-card image of St. Martín surrounded by the dog, the cat, and the mouse interpreted by the key sign of a white dove invites us to experience the wounds of the risen Christ in Lima, Peru. The holy-card image of St. Martín offers us the profound religious insight of the redemptive (and subversive) image of God. As such, this image participates, in a sense, in the Atonement achieved by Christ. It is an example of the human aspect of the Atonement. It is the ultimate transformation of a great evil into the great spiritual power of a wounded innocence embodied in the image of a marginalized mulatto that also represents a suffering America. It is a *felix culpa,* indeed.

1. The essential difference in my understanding between a community and a culture is that community involves an intentional and deliberate process, a "work," while culture involves a complex process where intentionality and deliberation are difficult to pin down. Thus, it is more natural to speak of a cultural "product" rather than a "work."

Community, in other words, refers to a social process that allows creativity. Community allows the indeterminacy that belongs to the freedom of spirit. At the same time, community by its spiritual nature is also personal and intentional. Indeed, community is a spiritual social process. By community, I also am thinking of an ancient characterization (actually Cicero's) of culture as *cultura animi.* Community cultivates whereas culture produces. Cultivation is an apt term for a social spiritual process. As such, community cultivates humanity. Community cultivates the full potential of our humanity that it may grow and give fruit.

2. David Morgan, *Visual Piety: A History and Theory of Popular Religious Images* (Berkeley, Calif.: University of California Press, 1998) 2.

3. Elaine Scarry sees an even worse dualism, the beautiful versus the sublime. She makes a case that Kant's distinction between the beautiful and the sublime undermines the dimension of justice present in art. Indeed, the distinction between the beautiful and the sublime corresponds to the distinction between the passionate and the contemplative. Elaine Scarry, *On Beauty and Being Just* (Princeton, N.J.: Princeton University Press, 1999).

4. Elizabeth Clark tells us that the iconoclastic dispute among the desert monks took place at the same time a campaign to eradicate Egyptian paganism was instigated by Bishop Theophilus in the 390s. Elizabeth A. Clark, *The Origenist Controversy: The Cultural Construction of an Early Christian Debate* (Princeton, N.J.: Princeton University Press, 1992) 55.

5. Lest the reader begin to think such a prayer is iconoclastic, Merton also saw images and, specially, art as the "means to enter more deeply into the life of prayer and meditation." Thomas Merton, *Contemplative Prayer* (Garden City, N.Y.: Image Books, 1971) 89, as quoted in Morgan, op. cit., 30.

6. Clark, op. cit., 54.

7. Sarapion's cry haunts me. For I have heard it from many simple folk who lament the loss of their beloved statues taken away from their places in the iconoclastic fervor that swept the Church after Vatican II. Unlike Sarapion, these folks were not Anthropomorphites. Their fervor, as we shall see, was thoroughly a Christian one. The real heresy lay with an iconoclasm that can't tell the difference between the human basis of faith and the holy presence of the Divine. John Cassian and Boniface Ramsey, *John Cassian, The Conferences,* translated by Boniface Ramsey, Ancient Christian Writers (New York: Paulist Press, 1997) X.III.5.

8. Cassian and Ramsey, op. cit., X.VI.3.

9. Ibid., X.VI.1.

10. Ibid., X.VI.2.

11. Here the following passage from Donald Gelpi is helpful. "Any theologian needs a sense of humor when it comes to God-talk. The ultimate reality of God will always elude adequate expression in finite human speech. At the same time, one can overstress the otherness of God.... A God so totally other as to have no point of analogous resemblance with creation defies revelation in space and time. The fact that God has in fact chosen to reveal and communicate the divine reality to mortals within space and time falsifies that extreme conception of divine otherness." Donald L. Gelpi, *The Gracing of Human Experience: Rethinking the Relationship Between Nature and Grace* (Collegeville, Minn.: The Liturgical Press, 2001) 358.

12. Some of these works include María Pilar Aquino and Roberto S. Goizueta, *Theology Expanding the Borders,* The Annual Publication of the College Theology Society (Mystic, Conn.: Twenty-Third Publications College Theology Society, 1998); Allan Fuigeroa Deck, ed., *Frontiers of Hispanic Theology* (Maryknoll, N.Y.: Orbis Books, 1992); Virgilio P. Elizondo, *Guadalupe, Mother of the New Creation* (Maryknoll, N.Y.: Orbis Books, 1997); Virgilio Elizondo, "Our Lady of Guadalupe as a Cultural Symbol," in *Liturgy and Cultural Traditions,* eds. Herman Power and David Schmidt (N.Y.: Seabury Press, 1977) 25–33; Orlando. Espín, *The Faith of the People Theological Reflections on Popular Catholicism* (Maryknoll, N.Y.: Orbis Books, 1997); Orlando Espín, "Religiosidad popular: unaporte para su definición y hermenéutica," *Estudios Sociales* 17 (October–December 1984) 41–54; Roberto S. Goizueta, *We Are a People: Initiatives in Hispanic American Theology,* edited by Roberto S. Goizueta (Minneapolis: Fortress Press, 1992).

13. See for example, Antonello Gerbi, *The Dispute of the New World: The History of a Polemic, 1750–1900,* translation of: *La disputa del Nuovo Mono: Storia di una polemica, 1750–1900,* original work published in Italy, 1955, translated and revised by Jeremy Moyle (Pittsburgh: University of Pittsburgh Press, 1973); Lewis Hanke, *Aristotle*

and the American Indians: A Study in Race Prejudice in the Modern World (Bloomington, Ind.: Indiana University Press, 1959); Anthony Pagden, *The Fall of Natural Man: The American Indian and the Origin of Comparative Ethnology,* reprint, 1982, Cambridge Iberian and Latin American Studies (Cambridge: Cambridge University Press, 1986); Antonello Gerbi, *The Dispute of the New World: The History of a Polemic, 1750–1900,* Translation of: *La disputa del Nuovo Mono: Storia di una polemica, 1750–1900,* original work published in Italy, 1955, translated and revised by Jeremy Moyle (Pittsburg: University of Pittsburgh Press, 1973); Lewis Hanke, *Aristotle and the American Indians: A Study in Race Prejudice in the Modern World* (Bloomington, Ind.: Indiana University Press, 1959); Anthony Pagden, *The Fall of Natural Man: The American Indian and the Origin of Comparative Ethnology,* Cambridge Iberian and Latin American Studies (Cambridge: Cambridge University Press, 1986) 1982.

14. By Latin Church of the Americas, I mean the ecclesial tradition born out of the missionary efforts of the Roman Catholic Church in the sixteenth century in the Americas and the faith of those who heard and believed the message of the Gospel preached not only in words but also by a way of life. This ecclesial tradition finds its home and is one with the wider tradition of the entire Roman Catholic Church but expresses this one tradition in her own American way. A fuller discussion is found in Alex García-Rivera, *The Community of the Beautiful: A Theological Aesthetics* (Collegeville, Minn.: The Liturgical Press, 1999) ch. 2.

15. Louis M. Colonnese and Catholic Church, *The Church in the Present-Day Transformation of Latin America in the Light of the Council Second General Conference of Latin American Bishops, Bogotá, 24 August, Medellin, 26 August–6 September, Colombia, 1968* (Bogota: General Secretariat of CELAM, 1970) 121.

16. Louis M. Colonnese and Catholic Church, *The Church in the Present-Day Transformation of Latin America in the Light of the Council Second General Conference of Latin American Bishops, Bogotá, 24 August, Medellin, 26 August–6 September, Colombia, 1968* (Bogota: General Secretariat of CELAM, 1970) 122.

17. Gustavo Gutiérrez, "Prologue," in *Religión del Pobre y Liberación en Chimbote,* edited by Diego Irarrazaval (Lima: Centrod de Estudios y Publicaciones, 1978) 7.

18. Diego Irarrazaval, "Cristianos en el Proceso Socialista," in *Cristianos por Socialismo,* edited by Reues Mate Ruperez (Estella: Editorial Verbo Divino, 1975) 466.

19. Father Virgilio Elizondo, a famous theologian and former rector of San Fernando Cathedral in San Antonio, Texas, is fond of telling this story. A young priest was proudly proclaiming to an *abuela,* an old but venerable long-time member of the church, how he had "cleaned up" the church from its statues and left in their place this sole magnificent crucifix. "Now the people will know," he said to the *abuela,* "who they are really worshipping." The *abuela* responded: "Yes, dear father, you are right but have you considered how lonely you have left our poor Lord?"

20. Goizueta's account in the chapter on "Beauty or Justice?" in Roberto S. Goizueta, *Caminemos con Jesús: Toward a Hispanic/Latino Theology of Accompaniment* (Maryknoll, N.Y.: Orbis Books, 1995).

21. Many of these stories were told at his beatification process. Many of these stories are retold in popular devotional books such as *San Martin de Porres,* vol. 1 of *Bilioteca Hombres del Peru,* edited by Hernan Alva Orlandini (Lima: La Oficina Tecnica Editorial de Edif. Caucato, 1964); Bernardo de Medina, O.P., *San Martin de Porres: Biografía del Siglo XVII,* reprint, 1663 (Mexico City: Editorial Jus, S.A., 1964); Neri

Romero de Pacchioni, *La Fascinante Vida del Santo Martín de Porres* (Lima: Centro de Proyección Cristiana, n.d.). The actual stories, however, can be found in the official documents of the beatification process. Secretariado Martín de Porres, translation from the Latin into Spanish of the official process of beatification of St. Martin of Porres during the years 1660–1674 in *Proceso de Beatificación de Fray Martín de Porres,* reprint, 1660–71 (Palencia: Secretatiado "Martin de Porres," 1960).

22. This story and the others retold in this chapter about St. Martin are translated by me from the official documents of the beatification process. Secretariado Martín de Porres, op. cit.

23. This is the conclusion of my previous work on St. Martin de Porres. Alex García-Rivera, *St. Martín de Porres the "Little Stories" and the Semiotics of Culture,* Faith and Cultures Series (Maryknoll, N.Y.: Orbis Books, 1995).

24. Mary Alphonsus, *St. Rose of Lima: Patroness of the Americas* (Rockford, Ill.: Tan Books and Publishers, 1968) 57.

25. This was transparent to the people in the times of St. Martin. His biographer, Bernardo de Medina, O.P., interpreted this story of the dog, the cat, and the mice in this way: "And thus [with this sight] it seemed God wanted to honor his servant with the prowess prophesied of his first coming by the prophet Isaias [Isa 11:6] who told of the coming together of many definite brutes, the wolf and the lamb, and the goat with the leopard *(pardo);* for here the same fellowship took place, if not goat and irrational leopard *(pardo irracional),* at least dogs, cats, and mouse, by virtue of a rational Mulato *(Pardo racional),* who was the same Fray Martín." [My translation from the official documents of the beatification process.]

26. United States Catholic Conference, *The Catechism of the Catholic Church* (Vatican City: Libreria Editrice Vaticana, 1994) #1106.

27. United States Catholic Conference, *The Catechism of the Catholic Church* (Vatican City: Libreria Editrice Vaticana, 1994) #1107.

28. Some of this history can be found in Robert Ricard, *The Spiritual Conquest of Mexico,* originally published in French as *Conquête Spirituelle de Mexique,* published as volume XX of *Travaux et Mémoires de L'institute d'Ethnologie* by the University of Paris, translated by Lesley Bird Simpson, California Library Reprint (Berkeley: University of California Press, 1966).

29. Most Christians know about the doctrine of Atonement either in its penal or in its "scapegoat" form. These two forms were worked out in the Middle Ages by various theologians, among them Anselm and Albert the Great. Even then, however, theologians such as Aquinas found difficulty with them. Today, the "scapegoat" form of the doctrine of Atonement was secularized by René Girard in the form of an overarching theory of social psychology. In any case, these two forms of the doctrine of Atonement leave much unclear. They do help explain the radical nature of evil but they are less helpful in explaining the dignity of the human creature. Indeed, in our day, it is not the evil that people make that needs to be explained. What needs to be explained is that, in spite of such evil, people are still capable of truth, goodness, and, yes, beauty. There are some very fine books detailing the history and theology of the Atonement. Among them are: Robert H. Culpepper, *Interpreting the Atonement* (Grand Rapids, Mich.: Eerdmans, 1966); Donald L. Gelpi, *Doctrinal and Practical Christology*, vol. 3 of *The Firstborn of Many: A Christology for Converting Christians,* Marquette Studies in Theology (Milwaukee: Marquette University Press, 2001) ch. 10; Timothy Gorringe, *God's*

Just Vengeance: Crime, Violence, and the Rhetoric of Salvation, Cambridge Studies in Ideology and Religion (Cambridge/New York: Cambridge University Press, 1996); H. D. McDonald, *The Atonement of the Death of Christ in Faith, Revelation, and History* (Grand Rapids, Mich.: Baker Book House, 1985); Leopold Sabourin, *Rédemption Sacrificielle une Enquête Exégétique* ([Bruges]: Desclée de Brouwer, 1961); Anthony J. Tambasco, *A Theology of Atonement and Paul's Vision of Christianity* (Collegeville, Minn.: The Liturgical Press, 1991).

30. I do not wish to be misunderstood here. The human aspect of the Atonement, as I understand it, does not deny the unique role of our Lord in the doctrine of the Atonement. The Atonement is solely the work of Christ. The human aspect of the Atonement, however, is a participation in Christ's work of atoning not an addition.

"The Vietnam Veterans Memorial"

CHAPTER SIX

The Tyger and the Lamb

When the stars threw down their spears

And water'd heaven with their tears:
Did he smile his work to see?
Did he who made the Lamb make thee?

"The Tyger and the Lamb,"
William Blake[1]

Kant might have written a different philosophy of art if he had visited the Vietnam Veterans Memorial in Washington, D.C. Rather than a "disinterested pleasure," Kant would have seen people touching and crying, kneeling and saluting a work of art. In other words, not a disinterested judgment but a passionate involvement defines the aesthetics in this powerful memorial to the veterans of the Vietnam War. Kant missed the theological dimension in works of art. In particular, he was blind to the healing power that some works of art possess. The Vietnam Veterans Memorial is such a work of art. As such, the memorial, as a work of art, offers a religious insight into the way and need of salvation. This chapter explores the particular religious insight of the Vietnam Veterans Memorial. This insight, I believe, concerns a doctrine at the center of a tragic theological dispute known as the Reformation. I am speaking of the doctrine of justification.

The doctrine of justification, like Blake's "The Tyger" and "The Lamb," addresses the deep ambiguity inherent in human participation in sin. Luther pointed to this ambiguity in his famous Reformation battle cry: the human is *simul iustus et peccator,* "at once both sinner and justified." Such ambiguity also applies to the United States in the case of the Vietnam War. "The Tyger" and "The Lamb" speak of the deep ambiguity of the United States participation in the evil of the Vietnam

War. For some, Communist Vietnam was "The Tyger" and the United States was "The Lamb." For others, Communist Vietnam was "The Lamb" and the United States "The Tyger." In either case, the nation's unified experience was one of being ensnared in the heart of evil, an evil that deeply wounded every citizen that lived through this time in the nation's history. The experience, however, was not that half the nation was "Tyger" and the other half "Lamb." What the nation actually experienced was that it was both "Tyger" and "Lamb." As such, Blake's words name the artistic challenge facing the Vietnam Memorial. "Did he smile his work to see? Did he who make the Lamb make thee?"

The Vietnam Veterans Memorial, as a public, national work of art, faces a special challenge. It must express a special unity between the Lamb and the Tyger, between the innocence and the violence of a nation. Moreover, such unity must be one that heals and reconciles. The challenge lies in that such unity, a unity capable of reconciling the "Tyger" and the "Lamb," cannot be found in the character of the nation itself. Blake's poem places that special unity squarely on God. Only in God can "Tyger" and "Lamb" be said to have a real relationship. Theologically speaking, Blake's poem tells us that only he who made both the Lamb and the Tyger can also be he in whom the deep ambiguities of sin and evil can find healing and reconciliation. Thus, the artistic challenge in the Vietnam Veterans Memorial.

The dual role of the United States in the Vietnam War cannot find a unity solely on the resources of the nation's history or character itself. Neither patriotism nor the sacralizing of the nation's character will help find the unity the memorial tries to achieve. Indeed, healing and reconciliation cannot come from the nation itself. It must find a higher power. In other words, the artistic challenge of the Vietnam Veterans Memorial concerns the healing of a divided nation that involves a presence both *coram Deo* and *coram hominibus,* before the presence of a higher power and before the hopeful and watchful eyes of the public. Blake's poem points to the direction such an aesthetic must take. It is that region of the heart that lies between "Tyger" and "Lamb." It is the region of a wounded innocence.

The Vietnam Memorial

I served in Vietnam myself and this is one thing I wanted to see while I was here. It seems all the names strike you as the fact that human life was sacrificed, just like I saw when I served—but the nation didn't support it. It makes you think, why did all these men die, and literally in vain?

—James Lewis

Five of my boys are on the wall. Three of the five were my students. Stanley Bradley was my student in 1956 in Georgia when I was teaching the seventh grade there. His feet wouldn't even reach the floor. . . . The father was a judge, and he was sitting on the bench, and the moment the officers walked in he said he knew why they were there. And he wrote Mr. Nixon and said, "Why? Why my son?"

— Phyllis Fisher

I've got four kids and I'm trying to get a disability from the government, I've got Agent Orange real bad on my legs and my arms. Do you know they've got a big warehouse full of the stuff people have left at the wall, and that there's been a dozen guys guns to their heads at night, and the vets have talked them out of it? And the wall weeps. Water comes down on the letters and they disappear and there are those who say that water comes right out of the names.

— Gene Isaacs

If you can't see, you wouldn't think you would get much out of it, but you get much more than you would know. . . . When I went to the wall I asked someone to put my hand on their names, I got a gut feeling—John and I were kind of close—when I put my hand there I said, "John, I am touching you again."

— Gerald Fulkerson (who is blind)[2]

When I was pondering what work of art might shed light on the doctrine of justification, a couple of my students talked me out of considering works from the Reformation period.[3] They suggested that instead of looking at a painting by Cranach or an engraving by Dürer, I should take a look at the Vietnam Veterans Memorial. As I researched the "Wall," I was struck by their brilliant insight.[4] The Vietnam Memorial was conceived as a realistic but sensitive response to the memory of those who died fighting a war that, ultimately, many saw as immoral or unnecessary. As the testaments above suggest, many names written on the Wall witnessed a journey from a kind of idealistic innocence to a profound sense of betrayal by the nation they idealized. An encounter with the Wall is an encounter with evil and sin on a national level. It is also an encounter with the possibility of a renewed innocence. Is it possible to justify the deaths (and lives) of these men and women? Is it possible for a nation to confess its sins and find forgiveness and reconciliation? Is it possible to believe in the possibility of a better world as one faces the names written on this black marble stone? For a theologian, these questions are the stuff of the doctrine of justification and few Reformation works of art deal with it in as direct and powerful way as the Vietnam Veterans Memorial.

Jan Scruggs, a veteran of the Vietnam War, saw the movie *The Deer Hunter* in March 1979. The movie artistically explored the journey from innocence to cynicism and back to a chastened innocence of a tightly knit group of soldiers raised in the same small town in Pennsylvania. In the movie, the local boys, shattered by the horrors of their experience in the war, return to their town only to find that the war has changed them. What was once a tight community now reflects the shattered innocence of its returning sons. The movie continues to show a community reeling to find a past innocence. They do so by trying to return to the patriotic ideals that first inspired their ready commitment to send their own citizens to war. In the end, *The Deer Hunter* successfully conveys a gracious forgiveness and reconciliation that returns the community to a new kind of innocence, chastened and wounded, but also able to dream of ideals again.[5]

Jan Scruggs was so moved by the movie that he formed the Vietnam Veterans Memorial Fund (VVMF) in April of 1979. The VVMF aimed to build a memorial that emphasized the lives (and deaths) of the soldiers rather than the federal government. The VVMF wanted a *veterans* memorial rather than a *war* memorial. For these reasons, they refused federal monies and sought only private donations. The funding for the $10 million project came in slowly at first but after a couple of years, significant donations poured in. The VVMF had struck a nerve in the nation's own need for a significant Vietnam Memorial. One of the key decisions made by the VVMF was also its most powerful artistic elements. The memorial would list *all* the names of those killed, missing in action, or still held as prisoners of war in Vietnam.[6] The decision provided the Vietnam Veterans Memorial with its first artistic challenge.

The second artistic challenge came in the directive given in 1981 to a panel of jurors that would choose the best design for the memorial. Jan Scruggs charged the panel to find the design of a memorial that would "begin healing process, a reconciliation of the grievous divisions wrought by the war."[7] More than 1,400 designs were submitted to the panel. On May 1, 1981, the jurors chose a remarkable design by Maya Ying Lin, a Chinese-American woman who was a 21-year-old student at Yale. Her design would prove to be one of the most artistically powerful funerary monuments in recent U.S. history.[8]

Lin's design sensitively and brilliantly dealt with the key element of listing the names of the Vietnam veterans who had died or were imprisoned in the war. Simply listing them alphabetically would have given the memorial a kind of "phone book" homogeneity. Lin decided to list the names of the men and women in the order in which they had died. Each name embodied a personal history that now would be carved into the black granite stone that came from Bangalore, India. Thus, Lin gave each name a strong personal presence in the stone by virtue of its position. Moreover, each name was carved in such a way as to give a strong physical presence. Carved into the granite, the names cry out to be touched or to be taken home by the visitor by making a rubbing of the name.

The black granite itself makes an artistic statement. It is intentionally polished to be as reflective as a mirror. As the visitor reads the names, he or she sees their own face on the wall. The reflection offers a deep ambiguity. On the one hand, solidarity with the dead could not be made more explicitly. On the other hand, it also suggests the beholder's own participation in the tragedy of the war. The mirror surface not only invites compassion for the dead but also judges the living. The black granite rises out of the ground at two places forming a "V" that reaches a height of nine to ten feet. Thus as one walks towards the apex reading names, the walls (and the names) of the memorial rise above one's head giving a sense of being overwhelmed by all the names. The "V" design also leads the visitor from a very public space to an eerily private space at the very apex. What strikes the beholder at this point is the experience of seeing one's own face reflected amidst a sea of names in a very private (and lonely) space. Such experience is the stuff of the confessional. Maya Lin may not have had the intention of making a theological statement with her design. Nonetheless, a theological dimension is powerfully present. I will say more about this below.

In spite of its spiritual power, the Vietnam Veterans Memorial stirred a lot of protest. Maya Lin's design was called "a black gash of shame and sorrow," "a wailing Wall for future anti-draft and anti-nuclear demonstrators," "an Orwellian glob," and "a tribute to Jane Fonda."[9] As a theologian, I see Maya Lin's Vietnam Veterans Memorial as possessing a profound religious insight into the need and the way of salvation.

The Religious Insight

The Wall's mirror-polished surface reminds me of a passage from Dante's *Purgatorio*. In Canto Nine, Dante falls asleep and awakens before Peter's Gate and a series of three steps that lead into purgatory proper. "There we came, and the first step was white marble so smooth and polished that I could see my reflection in it. The second step was darker than bluish-black, of rough and scorched stone, crossed with two great cracks. The third and highest step, which was massive, seemed to be of porphyry stone that flamed as red as any blood that spurts from a vein."[10] Kathryn Lindskoog explains the symbolic meaning for these steps: "The first part of penitence is confession. The penitent person sees himself as he is, a sinner, and honestly confesses. The second part of penitence is contrition (grief for sin). . . .The third part of penitence is restitution. This includes an appropriation of Christ's sacrifice for the sins of the world, and a pouring out of one's own life and love."[11]

Maya Lin's Wall, I believe, encompasses the qualities of these three "steps" of Dante's *Purgatorio*. Its mirror surface, intended to act as a mirror, resembles the first element of the first step. As mirror, the Wall offers a certain ambiguity. It expresses a certain solidarity with the dead. Our face, after all, appears amidst the names. On the other hand, the very flow of the Wall invites an inner, contemplative gaze that involves a tragic dimension. This suggests that the mirror surface invites visitors to consider their own participation in the tragedy before them. Perhaps this is not exactly penitence or confession but it comes very close to it.

The blackness of the Wall resembles the second step. Though not cracked, it is as dark as the bluish-black (the traditional color for penitence) of Dante's step. Like this step, the blackness of the Wall evokes grief. Here another ambiguity presents itself. Does the Wall invite us to grieve or, like, Gene Isaacs mentions, is it the Wall itself that grieves? In either case, the Wall certainly has the dimension of grief that has both an internal dimension proper to the memorial itself as well as an external dimension that addresses grief in the beholder. The blackness of the Wall also suggests a certain sinfulness. This Wall is no heroic paean to a righteous victory. It is, however, an invitation to face squarely a tragic misstep in a nation's history.

There is no scarlet red on the Wall, and perhaps here the analogy with Dante fails. Nonetheless, though the red is not seen it is certainly felt. The very names on the Wall speak of sacrifice, and sacrifice given in blood. Moreover, the Wall evokes a response in us of leaving a little of ourselves behind, a kind of sacrificial offering. By 1993 the National Park Service had collected over 250,000 objects ranging from the extremely personal to the mass-produced. Even the mass-produced, however (bottles of booze, for example), speak of a very personal exchange. Something about the Wall invites a gesture that is the nature of a sacrifice.

The analogy of the Wall with Dante's steps to purgatory does not come close to being exact. As such, the Wall offers a religious insight. Those who are moved by the Wall's artistry are moved into a recognition of their own need of salvation. Such is the stuff of the doctrine of justification.[12]

The Reformation and the Vietnam Veterans Memorial

The doctrine of justification was the center of an internal theological conflict (the Reformation) similar to the internal conflict between citizens of the United States. Like the national internal conflict caused by the Vietnam War, the Reformation pitted brother against brother, sister against sister, family against family. The Reformation polarized people to the same degree, if not more, as the Vietnam conflict. I know this as a living fact for it still affects my family. I am a former Lutheran pastor that returned to his original baptismal roots of Roman Catholicism. I returned, in no small part, because I was convinced of the truth and wisdom of the Roman Catholic position on the doctrine of justification. The return came at a personal price. My wife remained Lutheran and we both attend different churches. The centuries-old division continues to haunt my family to this day. Having said that, I also believe that much of the controversy and the subsequent tragedy concerning this doctrine revolves around a theological aesthetic that has not been fully appreciated. Language has been, indeed, the stumbling block that prevents reconciliation. The Vietnam Veterans Memorial speaks to my hope that such a reconciliation may one day be possible. Art may help theology overcome a doctrinal dispute in which language has failed.

The recent Joint Declaration on Justification by Lutheran and Roman Catholic theologians has only affirmed this conviction. The doctrine of justification attempts to understand the nature of the forgiveness and reconciliation of a sinful human creature. Justification attempts to answer the question: what, exactly, does it mean for God to say, "Your sins have been forgiven"? In the sixteenth century, a furious dispute arose over various answers to this question. The dispute led to a tragic division in the Christian community. Since the 1970s scholars in the Lutheran and Roman Catholic communities suspected that language had much to do with the dispute. Based on this suspicion, these scholars have struggled to disentangle the semantic and linguistic understandings constituting the dispute. If language, in terms of differing philosophical presuppositions, had been the cause of the dispute, then language, in the form of an ecumenical dialogue, might be the answer. Thus, it was with great hope and expectations that the long and often frustrating work of ecumenical dialogue finally bore fruit. The Joint Declaration on Justification, the fruit of decades of intense theological discussion, was signed in Augsburg by the Roman Catholic Church and the Lutheran World Federation on Reformation Day, October 31, 1999.[13]

The document testifies at once to the power and the weakness of language in theology. I had hoped that the Joint Declaration on Justification would be a kind of Vietnam Veterans Memorial for a divided theological community. I had hoped that the Joint Declaration on Justification would have been a memorial to a long theological dispute. This has not been the case. Less than a memorial, the Joint Declaration on Justification witnesses less to a past event than a continuing conflict. Though a marvelous achievement of dialogue, the Joint Declaration, unfortunately, has not met a warm reception either in the Lutheran or the Roman Catholic communities. For all its success at disentangling linguistic misunderstandings, the document floundered on what Cardinal Avery Dulles called "two languages of salvation." It is obvious that language did not solve the nagging conflict that still divides these two communities.

Two Languages of Salvation

There are two related but distinct theological discourses on justification. They both concern evil.[14] One discourse is known as theodicy, which comes from the Greek *theos,* or "God," and *dikos,* or "justice." Theodicy concerns justifying God to the human in light of the evil that exists in the world. Theodicy attempts to answer the question: How can a good and all-powerful God allow evil to exist? It is the question implicit in Blake's poem: "Did He who make the Lamb make thee?" It is also one of the most difficult questions in theology. Justification itself, on the other hand, focuses on the relationship of evil to the human creature itself. The language of justification (both Lutheran and Roman Catholic) tends to place the human creature as one who stands before

God's perspective as responsible for the evil in the world. The human now must be justified before God.[15]

The justification of the human before God, however, depends, in no small part, on how one sees the justification of God to the human in light of the evil that exists. In other words, human righteousness depends on God's righteousness. Or, in the language of innocence, human innocence depends on God's innocence. In the context of evil, the relationship is full of tension. God's innocence extends to all his creation. The human creature made in the image of God was also made in the image of divine Innocence. If God is innocent, then so is his image. Yet, the inescapable conclusion persists. If God is innocent, then the only other creature capable of evil is the human, precisely because he and she are made in the image of God. The Christian answer to resolve this tension is as profound as it is simple. God is innocent, and the human guilty but because the human is beloved and made in the image of Innocence, the human must be made innocent as well.

This "making innocent," or "making just" in the Christian tradition takes place through the life, death, and resurrection of Jesus Christ. Christ becomes the Lamb that reconciles the human Tyger. It is Christ's life, death, and resurrection that allow the human creature to be "made just" or innocent again. It is Christ's righteousness that makes possible human righteousness. Making just or innocent, however, contains a certain ambiguity. Is it an event or a process? Does God declare us just in light of Christ's righteousness or does Christ's righteousness imply human participation in the life, death, and resurrection of Christ? Is Christ's righteousness something to be beheld by God for the benefit of the human creature or something to be achieved by the human creature by beholding the righteousness of Christ? Are we justified by Christ's righteousness and innocence or are we sanctified through it?

Almost five hundred years of tragic misunderstandings and conflicts separate Christians over this powerful ambiguity. The Joint Declaration on Justification has come a long way towards resolving the ambiguity but, in the final analysis, I do not believe it succeeded. Cardinal Dulles correctly points out the main stumbling block in the Joint Declaration on Justification. There still exists "two languages" of salvation in the Joint Declaration.[16] By two languages, he means the related but distinct discourses that accompany the doctrine of justification, namely, the language of justification and the language of sanctification. Both revolve around our understanding of the role Christ's righteousness plays in the reconciliation of the Tyger and the Lamb.

The Aesthetic Dimension in the Two Languages of Salvation

The dispute over the doctrine of justification can be summarized in terms of presence.[17] The language of justification per se concerns being "justified," *coram Deo,* before the presence of God. As such, it corresponds to the Lutheran insight into the doctrine of justification. It is Christ's righteousness that is solely responsible for our being made just. God beholds Christ's innocence and forgives us our sins. Luther, however, pushed this doctrinal truth to its limit. For him, human righteousness simply did not exist. As a consequence, Christ's righteousness is a *iustitia aliena,* an "alien justice" to the human. No righteousness is possible to the human except as a righteousness not truly their own but only belonging to Christ's. Such a way of putting it emphasizes the true religious insight that human justification is solely possible only because of Christ's righteousness. Unfortunately, it also makes impossible the possibility of human participation in that righteousness in an incarnational way.

The language of sanctification, on the other hand, concerns "being justified," *coram hominibus,* before the presence of a community of men and women. The Church responded to Luther's *iustitia aliena* by emphasizing the continuity between being forgiven and being transformed, between the event of justification and the process.[18] If a sinner repents, and finds forgiveness, doesn't that mean a visible change in the lifestyle of the forgiven? If sin and lifestyle are intrinsically related, does not that mean that forgiveness and lifestyle are also similarly related? Sanctification, after all, concerns a way of living out a holy lifestyle. A holy lifestyle means the imitation of Christ. It means participating in the righteousness of Christ in such a way that our lifestyle reflects that righteousness. Such a lifestyle takes place in the public arena, i.e., *coram hominibus.*

Unfortunately, the Joint Declaration on Justification did not resolve this dispute. As Cardinal Dulles pointed out, two distinct languages of salvation remain. It is my observation that Cardinal Dulles (and the Joint Declaration) failed to appreciate the intrinsic aesthetic of these two "languages." Lifestyle relates to sin and forgiveness as the visible relates to the invisible. Lifestyle makes visible the invisible dimension of both sin and forgiveness. The forgotten dimension in the disputes over the doctrine of justification was its aesthetics. In other words, the doctrine of justification concerns not only the language of sin and forgiveness but also the vision of sin and forgiveness. Making just also means making visible the invisible. As such, the doctrine of justification also needs the language of art and aesthetics.

The aesthetics of justification becomes clearer in the intrinsic aesthetic dimension of *presence*. Presence, after all, suggests someone seeing someone else. For Luther, presence involved a one-way vision. Only God could truly "see" a sinner *rechtfertigung,* i.e., "made right." In response, the Roman Catholic position affirmed Augustine's position. Justification not only takes place *coram Deo* but also *coram hominibus,* not only before the gracious eyes of God but also before the watching and hopeful eyes of humanity itself.[19] Not only God but the community of men and women "see" the human transformation of a sinner to saint.[20] Perhaps the most tragic element in the entire Reformation dispute might be the crucial use of the language of presence without acknowledging its inherent aesthetic dimension.

The Vietnam Veterans Memorial, on the other hand, is quite aware of the aesthetics of presence. Its very aesthetics attempt to make present those who died in the Vietnam War. It does this, as we saw above, in various artistic ways. Moreover, the memorial's aesthetics of presence does not attempt to justify a war but reconcile a nation divided over it. It does so by making present the fallen in a way that heals, and, yes, justifies, those who survived. Indeed, the Vietnam Veterans Memorial has the nature of justification *coram hominibus*. If one looks deeper at the healing power of the memorial, however, one must come to the conclusion that the memorial also has a religious presence, a presence *coram Deo*. Here, I believe, lies the theological aesthetics of justification.

A Wounded Innocence

The great artistic question to be asked of the Vietnam Veterans Memorial, in my opinion, is: in what sense, does it heal? How do its artistic elements combine to provide an experience that is healing and reconciliatory? It is, in a sense, a therapeutic question, a question about psychological analysis and healing. Paul Tillich, the great Lutheran theologian, can help us to partly answer that question. Tillich was in constant dialogue with psychoanalysis.[21] He saw in Freud a certain realism that spoke to the disillusionment in a human ability to create a peaceful and rational world. Freud's analysis of neurotic behavior dispels any hope of an utopian world. Freud's psychoanalytic theories essentially place the site of human emancipation in the struggle for emancipation itself. Though Tillich liked much in Freud's theory of psychoanalysis, he saw analysis as insufficient in describing the human condition. The human condition is not only one of struggle but also one of hope and of vision of a struggle-less future.

Tillich proposed that the human condition is marked by three ever-present conditions in human nature. These include "essential goodness, existential estrangement and the possibility of something, a 'third,' beyond essence and existence, through which the cleavage is overcome and healed."[22] In other words, the human condition involves an integrating, dynamic process that begins with an untroubled unity which becomes disparate through conflict and, then, finally is reunited. This process becomes the basis to understand forgiveness and reconciliation. Through Tillich's eyes, then, this process accounts for the spiritual, healing power of the Vietnam Veterans Memorial. The process, however, hinges on a certain understanding of innocence.

The initial untroubled unity of Tillich's dynamic human condition belongs to what Tillich called a "dreaming innocence." Tillich uses it as a psychological term that depicts the state of Adam and Eve in Paradise. By "dreaming innocence," he refers to the "non-actualized potentiality" characteristic of dreams but now applied to human innocence before the Fall. As he puts it, "The word 'innocence' [like dreaming] also points to non-actualized potentiality. One is innocent only with respect to something which, if actualized, would end the state of innocence. The word has three connotations. It can mean lack of actual experience, lack of personal responsibility, and lack of moral guilt. In the metaphorical use suggested here, it is meant in all three senses. It designates the state before actuality, existence, and history."[23]

Tillich uses his proposal of a "dreaming innocence" to reinterpret the Fall. To do this, he gives us a psychological analogy.

> Up to a certain point, the child is unconscious of his sexual potentialities. In the difficult steps of transition from potentiality to actuality, an awakening takes place. Experience, responsibility, and guilt are acquired, and the state of dreaming innocence is lost. This example is evident in the biblical story, where sexual consciousness is the first consequence of the loss of innocence.[24]

Through this analogy, Tillich connects the Fall to human experience. The Fall is no longer something that happened in the past. It is something that describes the human condition. The Fall describes the loss of innocence as the very emergence of consciousness. It is, in a deep sense, the discovery of human autonomy as a kind of "awakening," a sense of inescapable guilt.[25] The "awakening" from a "dreaming innocence" brings to the human creature not only the gift of autonomous consciousness but also the curse of an unhappy consciousness.

Tillich's account of the Fall has the merit of a powerful strategy to deal with evil on a day-to-day basis. Tillich's "awakening" places the healing power of the Christian message in the "courage to be."[26] As such, the virtue of Tillich's account as an "awakening" from a "dreaming innocence" amounts to a reinterpretation of the doctrine of justification that goes beyond Luther's passive account. Reconciliation becomes an ever-present challenge, a matter of coping with one's own suffering. Somehow in that coping, God will also be found and in a marvelously gracious way make the suffering right. Tillich's account gives justification a dynamic, human element and brought it closer to earth. It also brings the presence of God into the presence of human suffering. In a brilliant way, Tillich somehow brings the twin presences of God and humanity into the doctrine of justification. As such, Tillich's account goes far in addressing the divide between justification and sanctification that Cardinal Dulles identified in the Lutheran and Roman Catholic positions.

The Vietnam experience, however, raises the question of the sufficiency of Tillich's account. It is not only the struggle with one's suffering that needs reconciliation but also the struggle with the memory of those who have suffered.[27] The veterans that come to the memorial not only face their own suffering but the memory of those who have suffered with them and are now gone. It is life itself that is the problem for these veterans. Life moves on and prevents them from being at the side of their dying friend. The guilt of the veteran is not the guilt of the "awakened." It is the guilt of the survivor.

As such, the guilt of the survivor revolves around the question of presence, or, rather, the lack of it. The guilt of the survivor involves the "sin" of having left a loved one behind. As such, the guilt of the survivor has analogy with the theological guilt of sin. The guilt of the survivor concerns remorse for an unjustified separation from a loved one. In a sense, such is the nature of theological guilt. In theological guilt, however, God is the loved one from whom we have separated. The removal of that guilt depends on reestablishing the relation broken by the separation. The Wall's power comes from its aesthetic ability to do that. When Gerald Fulkerson, the veteran quoted above, says "John, I am touching you again," he witnesses to the making new a relationship that death and time had broken.

The memorial's artistic power comes from its ability to bring presence to a broken relationship. Presence is the essential ingredient of the Wall's healing power. At this point one can ask about the therapeutic nature of the aesthetics of presence. Is the aesthetics of presence something that takes place in the psychological depths of the beholder? Or is the aesthetics of presence something that resides in the memorial itself? Does the healing process take place within the beholder? Or is it the art of the Wall itself that heals the beholder? Put this way, the insufficiency of the therapeutic explanation becomes self-evident. If healing takes place solely by the beholder's own powers, then the artistic contribution of the Wall becomes irrelevant. If the power to heal resides solely on the art of the Wall itself, then the aesthetic experience of the beholder becomes irrelevant.

The healing presence the Wall affords the beholder restates an ancient question about beauty. St. Augustine first articulated this aesthetic conundrum. Augustine put it: "Do beautiful things delight because they are beautiful or are they beautiful because they delight?"[28] The healing aesthetics of presence of the Vietnam Memorial restates the question in this manner. Does the healing presence of the Wall lie in its artistic contribution or in the aesthetic experience of the beholder? Put this way, the questions closely resemble the questions concerning the doctrine of justification. As such, they allow the theologian a certain insight not only into the nature of art but also into the nature of grace.

One begins taking a first step towards this insight by noting that presence is above all a relationship. Indeed, the healing presence of the Vietnam Veterans Memorial restores a broken relationship. Such, however, is the nature of grace as well. Grace has been called the "God-relation."[29] Grace as the "God-relation" makes the point that grace is less a "thing" than a relationship. Grace, however, is a very special relationship. Indeed, the nature of that relationship is what is at stake in the dispute over the doctrine of justification. The dispute could be put (simplistically) in the following manner: Is grace a one-way relationship between God and the human or is it a two-way relationship?

I believe this question can be approached through the language of art and aesthetics. The common term in the God-relation is creativity. Grace as God-relation is not simply the relation between God and the human but between Creator and creature. Put this way, grace can be seen as another way to ask the question of the *capax Dei*, the capacity of the finite human creature to know and love the infinite God. The relation, as such, cannot be a mere connectedness between God and the human. The God-relation is quite intimate. It is also a communion. Thus, a third term must be proposed to complete and describe the relationship. Let me suggest this third term to be creativity.

Creativity, I believe, takes us further into understanding the relationship between the infinite God and the finite creature because the Christian tradition gives strong support that human creativity derives from and subsists in divine creativity. Philip Hefner, director of the Chicago Center for Science and Religion, described this relationship of creativity as being "co-creators" with God. As such, human creativity amounts to a special kind of communion with the Divine life. Human creatures depend on God's creativity to create themselves anew. It is this continuity yet distinctiveness between human and divine creativity that makes the God-relation difficult to describe in either a one-way or two-way manner. The God-relation, in the context of creativity, is both. Human creativity depends on God's creativity but it also has its own integrity and dignity. Human creativity must be, after all, truly human.

Jacques Maritain, I believe, came very close to describing the nature of the relationship between divine and human creativity when he spoke of "creative intuition." What he has to say about "creative intuition" is worth quoting in full:

> In order that there should grow unceasingly, conforming to its law, the life of the creative spirit, it is necessary that the center of subjectivity where this creative spirit awakens to itself in suffering the things of the world and those of the soul should unceasingly be deepened. In following this line of reflection one would probably be led to ask oneself whether, beyond a certain degree of depth, this progress in spirituality can continue unless, under one form or another, a religious experience properly so called helps the soul of the poet to quit the surface levels.
>
> In any case, what I want to keep in mind here, is that creation takes form at different levels within the spiritual fabric of the soul—everyone by this very fact confesses what he is. The more the poet grows, the deeper the level of creative intuition descends into the density of his soul. Where formerly he could be moved to song, he can do nothing now, he must dig down deeper. One would say that the shock of suffering and vision breaks down, one after another, the living sensitive partitions behind which his identity is hiding. He is harassed, he is tracked down, he is destroyed. Woe to him if in retiring into himself he finds a heaven devastated, inaccessible; he can do nothing then but sink into his hell. But if at the end of the ends the poet turns silent, it is not that the growth of which I speak may ever come to an end, it is not that of itself the song does not still ask to be more deeply born in him, less distant

> from the creative untreated spirituality, archetype of all creative life: it is that the partition of the heart has been attained, and the human substance consumed.[30]

Maritain's description of the creative process, I believe, describes the healing aesthetics of presence experienced at the Vietnam Memorial.

As Maritain describes the process, creativity possesses both a negative and a positive dimension. Its positive dimension parallels in a striking way Tillich's proposal for grace. Creative intuition is an awakening "to itself in suffering the things of this world." As such, this element also parallels the initial experience of those who visit the memorial. Yet this is only one aspect of it. There exists a negative dynamic. Creativity deepens as "the shock of suffering and vision breaks down, one after another, the living sensitive partitions behind which his identity is hiding." A spiritual descent begins where custom and comfortable assumptions break down, indeed, are "destroyed." Finally, creativity reaches a dark but very creative place after all "human substance is consumed": the depths of the human "cave," the "partition of the heart."

This point in the creative process takes us to Dante's steps. Here one becomes aware of his own insufficiency. One faces the self mirrored on the darkness of her own suffering and sense of helplessness. As such, it is a moment akin to the confession of sin. It is also, like Tillich's insight, a moment for courage. One must find the courage to let go of the self and enter a mysterious but fertile place where something new and wondrous can happen. It is the place of the *coram Deo*. It is, indeed, the place of a mysterious but renewing Innocence.

As such, Maritain's description of the creative intuition also helps describe the dynamics of grace in terms of a creative relationship. Grace involves the forging of a relationship with God on the anvil of divine creativity. For the human creature, grace amounts to following the creative intuition to its deepest, most profound depths in order to encounter there the power and presence of a deeper creativity that grants the self the resources to fulfill the promise of a renewed innocence, the ability to dream, and trust, and hope anew.

Justification at the feet of the memorial, then, is not simply one's own suffering being made right. It is, as well, the grace of the creative intuition. It is the invitation to enter the process of human creativity applied to the wounds of a terrible suffering. It is the grace to be able to leave the sense of betrayal by a trusted nation, to leave the side of a dying friend and be open, once more, to the possibility of life, to dream of the possibility of a better world. As such, the healing grace of the memorial resembles Maritain's creative process. The veteran must search his or her soul to find the creative resources to put away the experience of betrayal, loss, separation, and lost innocence.

Part of the process of finding these resources is the paradoxical realization that one does not have the resources within themselves. This creative moment provides the analogy to what the theologian calls the forgiveness of sin. It amounts to entering the deepest part of one's soul only to find absent the resources needed to say, "I must go on." It is the engaging of the soul at its deepest part to become aware, once again, of a powerful innocence, an innocence that enables the soul to be open to a power greater than the self. Somehow, in its powerful aesthetics, the Wall engages the darkness of a spent soul in its openness through a newly found innocence and enables it to let go of the sins of the Vietnam experience and at last begin to truly live again.

The Vietnam Veterans Memorial exposes the aesthetics of justification not simply as the removal of guilt, nor the coping with personal suffering, but as a creative act that engenders the gift of life itself. As such, it is neither an artistic achievement nor an aesthetic experience but both. The gift of life emerges out of a creative act through which, as Walter Lowe explains, "one also by contrast clears a space—however distant, empty, and unattainable by one's own strength—in which innocence might abide."[31] The aesthetics of justification, in other words, is a wounded innocence. Its great insight is that at the heart of justification lies a mixing of divine and human creativity akin to the creativity in all great art. Such creativity opens up a space to the possibilities in life. It offers the renewal of vision and the impetus of a new lifestyle. The power of the Vietnam Veterans Memorial owes much of its ability to heal in its effectiveness in inviting a nation to confess its sins and be renewed by an innocence of vision, wounded and chastened, yes, but also life-giving and full of creative energy.

In the aesthetics of the Vietnam Veterans Memorial, the Lamb confronts the Tyger and both find a way to lie in peace with one another in the green meadow of a wounded innocence.

1. William Blake, "'The Tyger' and 'The Lamb,'" Web Page for Romantic Circles High School Reader containing William Blake's "The Tyger" and "The Lamb" from *Songs of Innocence and of Experience, copy Z* [London: Printed by Catherine Blake and William Blake, 1789–1794, 1826].

2. Excerpts from interviews published by Duncan Spencer and Lloyd Wolf, *Facing the Wall: Americans at the Vietnam Veterans Memorial* (New York/London: Macmillan Collier Macmillan, 1986).

3. The suggestion was raised as we conversed on a flight to Oakland after attending an American Academy of Religion conference in Denver. I want to thank Nancy Pineda-Madrid and Greg Zuschlag for their intellectual companionship. Their enthusiasm for scholarship renews my own intellectual journey. Very few things in life compare to the relationship between teacher and student. It has been my privilege to be mentor to many. I have also found that, in turn, they have been mentors to me.

4. The "Wall" refers to the Vietnam Memorial. It is the name many Vietnam veterans use to refer to the memorial.

5. Kristin Ann Hass, *Carried to the Wall: American Memory and the Vietnam Veterans Memorial* (Berkeley: University of California Press, 1998) 10.

6. The total number of names at the time of the proposal totaled fifty-eight thousand. Hass, op. cit., 13.

7. Jan C. Scruggs and Joel L. Swerdlow, *To Heal a Nation: The Vietnam Veterans Memorial* (New York: Harper & Row, 1985) 20.

8. Ironically, Lin got a "B" at her funerary architecture class at Yale for this exact design. Hass, op. cit., 15.

9. Hass, op. cit., 14–18.

10. This passage is quoted by the marvelous, readable translation given by Kathryn Lindskoog. Lindskoog makes Dante come alive for those not fluent in Italian. Her notes are marvelous and make the reading of Dante's *Divine Comedy* quite enjoyable and instructive. I also need to say that of all the three books by Dante, the *Purgatorio* is my favorite. I believe it has the most incisive understanding of the human condition. Kathryn Ann Lindskoog and Dante Alighieri, *Purgatory: Journey to Joy, Part Two*, vol. 2 of *Dante's Divine Comedy,* retold, with notes by Kathryn Lindskoog (Macon, Ga.: Mercer University Press, 1997) 50.

11. Lindskoog and Dante Alighieri, op. cit., n. 10, n. 11, n. 12 of Canto IX.

12. The reader might be interested in Alister McGrath's discussion of Dante's three steps in the history of the doctrine of justification. See, for example, Alister E. McGrath, *Iustitia Dei: A History of the Christian Doctrine of Justification* (Cambridge, U.K./New York: Cambridge University Press, 1998) 96ff.

13. Roman Catholic Church and Lutheran World Federation, "Joint Declaration on the Doctrine of Justification," online reference of full text of the Declaration and related Official Common Statement.

14. I must thank my dear friend and colleague, Donald Gelpi, S.J., for relating the question of evil and suffering to the doctrinal disputes on justification. I was struck by his account of the philosophical presuppositions that led to the dispute in his masterly, three-volume Christology. I must also stress, however, that the following account is my own and whatever errors or misinterpretations exist are mine and not his. I do recommend Professor Gelpi's fine account as found in Donald L. Gelpi, *Doctrinal and Practical Christology*, vol. 3 of *The Firstborn of Many: A Christology for Converting Christians,*

Marquette Studies in Theology (Milwaukee: Marquette University Press, 2001) 351–83.

15. In other words, the doctrine of justification is, at heart, an anthropodicy, justifying the human creature in the light of the evil they commit.

16. Avery Dulles, "Two Languages of Salvation: The Lutheran–Catholic Joint Declaration," *First Things* 98 (December 1999) 25–30.

17. See, for example, McGrath's exposition of the dispute in McGrath, op. cit., 198ff.

18. The language of conversion is helpful here to see this continuity. Justification concerns an initial conversion from sin to graced life and sanctification concerns an ongoing conversion. Donald L. Gelpi, *The Gracing of Human Experience: Rethinking the Relationship Between Nature and Grace* (Collegeville, Minn.: The Liturgical Press, 2001) 330ff.

19. McGrath, op. cit., 199ff.

20. In the dispute over justification, the question of "seeing" raises the specter of iconoclasm. Indeed, iconoclasm hangs as a shadow over the practice of many Reformation churches. Whether the language of vision is invoked or not, the subsequent iconoclasm that haunted many Reformation churches suggests that a theological aesthetics was at issue in the entire dispute. This suspicion only rises on noting that the Roman Catholic response, the Counter-Reformation, produced a tremendous spirit of art and aesthetic response. The real struggle in the Reformation, it seems to me, was not about "faith" versus "works" but about a new kind of iconoclasm that concerned the possibility of seeing the beauty of humanity itself.

21. Much of the following is a distillation from the insightful article by Professor Lowe. Walter James Lowe, "Innocence and Experience," in *Evil Self and Culture,* vol. 4, edited by Marie Coleman. Nelson and Michael Eigen, *Self-In-Process* (New York: Human Sciences Press, 1984) 248ff.

22. Paul Tillich, *Theology of Culture,* edited by Robert C. Kimball (New York: Oxford University Press, Galaxy, 1964) 119.

23. Paul Tillich, *Existence and the Christ,* vol. 2 of *Systematic Theology* (Chicago: University of Chicago Press, 1957) 34.

24. Ibid.

25. Lowe, op. cit., 250–51.

26. This is Tillich's most spiritual book. Many of his psychological insights into healing and reconciliation can be found there. Paul Tillich, *The Courage to Be,* Yale Nota Bene (New Haven, Conn.: Yale University Press, 2000).

27. Lowe, op. cit., 264.

28. Augustine, *De vera religione,* 32.

29. David H. Kelsey, "Human Being," in *Christian Theology: An Introduction,* edited by Alister E. McGrath (Oxford, U.K./Cambridge, Mass.: Blackwell, 1994) 182.

30. Jacques Maritain, *Creative Intuition in Art and Poetry,* A. W. Mellon Lectures in the Fine Arts (Princeton Guildford: Princeton University Press, 1977) 103–05.

31. Lowe, op. cit., 261.

"The Incredulity of St. Thomas"

CHAPTER SEVEN

A Wounded Innocence

An Epilogue

An early reader of the manuscript of this book asked me, "Alex, what you say about a wounded innocence is fascinating but can you tell me exactly what a wounded innocence means?" When I heard his question, I wondered if I had failed as a writer in conveying the meaning of the main theme of the book. But then I remembered I had heard this same critique before, namely, at the Museum of Modern Art in New York. A young man, obviously brought there against his better judgment by his girlfriend and looking at a painting (which painting I don't remember) asked with a mixture of confusion and annoyance the same question: "But what does it mean?" It struck me that perhaps my friend's question revealed not that I had failed but that somehow I had managed to take seriously one of the issues I had been wrestling with throughout the course of the book: *What would happen if we took the visual seriously in theology?*

The answer, judging from my friend's question, appears to be that this work of theology might not measure up as a textbook but succeed in exciting fascination and wonder. Nevertheless, I do take my friend's criticism seriously and someday I shall write that textbook that gives more precision to some of the themes in my writing but, for now, I shall opt to try to write theology that excites wonder and somehow touches the human heart and I would rather begin with that kind of theology because without first reaching such wonder, a textbook theology ought not to be attempted. A textbook, to be credible, should have taken the measure of the woundedness of language before it even begins to offer precision or definitions. Indeed, a textbook ought to make the woundedness of language the basis for its precision. For it is my conviction that the power of language lies not in its precision but rather in its woundedness.

In this sense, I do hope others will be able to say that, in this book, I have used the woundedness of language to great advantage in exploring the profound visual truths of the various works we looked at. As such, I also trust that the reader has experienced not only the woundedness of language but a woundedness transformed by the visual splendor of the works of art that began each chapter. I have aimed at involving the reader in the very struggle of expressing the theological dimension of art in order that the reader also experience something of that very creativity these pages have tried to describe. As such, I will be gratified if the reader discerns a grace beyond my own meager means, entering into the struggle and giving life to the words that mark its passing. Indeed, it is my fervent wish that the reader will be able to look with new eyes for a theological dimension that is present in all profound art. This, after all, was the main goal of these sketches. Thus, it seems fitting to me to end these brief sketches with one final work of art. This epilogue is intended as an answer to my friend's criticism: What precisely does a "wounded innocence" mean? I can only point, like John the Baptist, to a master work greater than this humble book, Caravaggio's *The Incredulity of St. Thomas.*[1]

Caravaggio's *Incredulity* bears striking resemblance to the cave painting of the "wounded hunter" that began these set of "sketches" or reflections on the theology of art. Echoing the visual elements of that profound painting in Lascaux, St. Thomas, like the "wounded hunter," in gritty realism that makes us wince, thrusts his finger deep into the wound in the side of Jesus in Caravaggio's *The Incredulity of St. Thomas.* Indeed, the powerful alignment of Jesus' and St. Thomas's hands together form a lance that thrusts once again into Jesus' side. St. Thomas's face expresses profound surprise as his finger thrusts deep into Jesus' wound. Perhaps, the surprise has to do with his unbelief. Yes, this is the Lord I saw dead and hanging on the cross. It could also be, however, surprise at the realization that he, too, is also pierced. Indeed, St. Thomas appears to clutch his side as if he becomes aware of a wound at his side as well. And we who wince at this gritty depiction feel a wound at our side as well. Caravaggio has masterfully captured through the hands of Jesus and Thomas the dynamics of a wounded innocence.

This "wounded innocence" continues to be explored through the means of light. We catch, for example, the apostles, all of them, at the instant of a certain kind of enlightenment, that which I have referred to in the book as a religious insight. Such insight is revealed dynamically in the uncovering by Jesus of the wound in his side. As Jesus' arm pulls his robe to uncover the wound at his side, it also enters a region of light as if the act of disrobing is identical with the act of revealing or enlightenment, or, in my view, insight. This same light also fills the faces of the apostles signaling the instant of a very special enlightenment. Jesus firmly guiding St. Thomas's finger into his wound gives support to that impression. Jesus, the wounded, becomes as well the Teacher. And we who contemplate Caravaggio's gritty realistic depiction of this profound encounter are also drawn into that instant. For we not only wince at the thrust of the finger but also sense that something has been revealed; we sense a moment of insight in the felt presence of a living woundedness and, as such, the insight becomes more than mere enlightenment but also redemptive. St. Thomas's poking into Jesus' wound reveals in a way no textbook could, the human need for salvation and also the way of that salvation.

If St. Thomas expresses surprise, the other apostles' faces register something else. Wonder shapes the faces of the other two apostles. But it is wonder whose striking reference is a marvelous woundedness. Indeed, Jesus' wound is placed near the center of the composition and the heads of the apostles, St. Thomas and Jesus hover over the wound in the shape of the cross, the apostles' faces express a marvelous wonder. But, what, is the source of that wonder? Is the wound itself? Let me suggest, it is suggested in the interlacing of Jesus' guiding hand and Thomas's thrusting finger. Jesus' body after all is no ordinary body. It is what theology calls the "glorious" or spiritual body of the resurrected. To touch or aesthetically explore that body requires not only the ordinary sensibilities of the physical body but also the sensibilities of the human spirit; and in the resurrection, then, both sensibilities must be as one.

The risen Jesus "teaches" Thomas to sense anew through the union of his physical and spiritual senses. This is the meaning, I think, of Jesus' sure and guiding hand on Thomas's physical and seeking finger. Jesus teaches Thomas the possibilities of a full humanity, the possibilities of a united physical and spiritual sensibility, the guiding hand of a risen but wounded body. Indeed, it is the wound at the side of Jesus that, in Caravaggio's painting, becomes the site where that union takes place. And, it is here, as well, that the mystery and the profundity of a wounded innocence takes shape and meaning.

It is true that the wound at Jesus' side refers to a terrible and awesome guilt, but it is also a wound borne by a risen Jesus. Whatever the guilt is that is referred by the wound, the wound, in the light of the resurrection, now refers to a marvelous innocence. Indeed, it is the reference to a horrendous guilt that allows us to see the presence of a wondrous innocence. And the transition from the fear and anguish of an unbearable guilt to the surprise and wonder of a redemptive innocence is the transition of a hesitant and uncertain sensibility to the sure and strong thrust of a guided and graced sensibility, a thrust that goes deep into the woundedness of our very humanity. Only a tremendous powerful innocence is capable of such a feat. This powerful innocence stands before St. Thomas as the Innocent One, the Lamb of God. And this Lamb takes this doubting, guilty Tyger into the heart of such innocence endowing him with the gift of a very special insight that is at the same time the result of a new sensibility. As such, the sign (and result) of an exquisite, spiritually physical sensibility is a wounded innocence. To be more precise than this is, perhaps, to work against that innocence. For it is not in precision where a wounded innocence is to be known but in the grace of a religious insight.

Thus, I find in Caravaggio's *Incredulity of St. Thomas* an answer to my friend's question. Caravaggio's fine work also reflects my own spiritual journey in writing this book. Like the apostles huddled in fear after the Lord's crucifixion, I experienced a few dark nights of the soul as I left my laptop in the evening after a day of writing and rewriting. I felt as a trespasser might who had jumped the fence over to his neighbor's property. What was this theologian doing in the properties of the art historian and art critic, of the artist and the art gallery? Yet as I struggled with the issues of these difficult disciplines, the work of art always took me deeply into what seemed a familiar field, a common ground in which there were no fences. This field was the heart of my own humanity in which I glimpsed a mysterious Beauty that transcended all fences, all methodological issues, and all claims. Here on the common ground of the beautiful, the theologian has a place along with the art historian and the critic, the artist and the museums for it is a common humanity that binds us. Whatever the wounds of history have done to isolate and separate the theological from the historical, the spiritual from the artistic, or the textbook from the living, a new humanism, a wounded innocence, I have come to believe, can bring them together.

1. Michelangelo Merisi, better known as Caravaggio, was born in a small town of the same name in the province of Bergamo, just east of Milan. Born in 1571, he died in 1610. Caravaggio shocked the art world of his day by his gritty realism. He used ordi-

nary people rather than idealized human bodies to depict sacred scenes. As such, his paintings offended the sensibilities of many that saw the Gospel stories as something that ought to be idealistically visualized rather than realistically depicted. I suspect that preference for the idealized rather than the gritty has its origin in a preference by churchmen for lofty doctrine over pastoral grittiness. Caravaggio, however, managed to combine the two in his paintings and, thus, became one of my favorite painters. Those interested in reading more about Caravaggio might consult Bernard Berenson, *Caravaggio, His Incongruity and His Fame* (London: Chapman & Hall, 1953); Howard Hibbard, *Caravaggio* (New York: Harper & Row, 1983); R. P. Hinks, *Michelangelo Merisi da Caravaggio: His Life, His Legend, His Works* (New York: Beechhurst Press, 1953); Peter Robb, *M the Man Who Became Caravaggio* (New York: Henry Holt, 2000).

Bibliography

Aertsen, Jan. *Medieval Philosophy and the Transcendentals the Case of Thomas Aquinas*. Studien und Texte Zur Geistesgeschichte Des Mittelalters. Leiden/New York: E. J. Brill, 1996.

Alexander, Thomas M., and John Dewey. "John Dewey's Theory of Art, Experience, and Nature the Horizons of Feeling." In *Classical American Pragmatism: Its Contemporary Validity*. SUNY Series in Philosophy. Albany, N.Y.: State University of New York Press, 1987.

Alphonsus, Mary. *St. Rose of Lima: Patroness of the Americas*. Rockford, Illinois: Tan Books and Publishers, 1968.

Aquino, María Pilar, and Roberto S. Goizueta. *Theology Expanding the Borders*. The Annual Publication of the College Theology Society. Mystic, Conn.: Twenty-Third Publications College Theology Society, 1998.

Balthasar, Hans Urs von. *Seeing the Form*. Vol. 1 of *The Glory of the Lord*. San Francisco/New York: Ignatius Press/Crossroad Publications, 1983.

———. "Theology and Sanctity." In *The Word Made Flesh*, vol. 1. Explorations in Theology, 181–209. San Francisco: Ignatius Press, 1989.

Balthasar, Hans Urs von, and John Kenneth. Riches. "Dionysius." In *Studies in Theological Style: Clerical Styles*. Vol. 2 of *The Glory of the Lord*, edited by John Kenneth Riches, translated by John Kenneth Riches. San Francisco/New York: Ignatius Press/Crossroad, 1984.

Barasch, Moshe. *Icon Studies in the History of an Idea*. New York: New York University Press, 1992.

Barth, Karl. "The Architectural Problem of Protestant Places of Worship." In *The Christian Place of Worship*, edited by Andre Bieler. Edinburgh and London: Oliver and Boyd, 1965.

Beckett, Wendy. *Art and the Sacred the Mystical Now*. New York: Universe, 1993.

Benton, John F. "Introduction: Suger's Life and Personality." In *Abbot Suger and Saint-Denis a Symposium*, edited by Paula Lieber Gerson. New York: Metropolitan Museum of Art, 1986.

Berenson, Bernard. *Caravaggio, His Incongruity and His Fame.* London: Chapman & Hall, 1953.
Bernard (of Clairvaux). *Apologia Ad Guillelmum Abbatrem*. In *Sancti Bernardi Opera*. Edited by Jean Leclercq and H. M. Rochais. Rome, 1957–77.
Bernstein, J. M. *The Fate of Art: Aesthetic Alienation from Kant to Derrida and Adorno*. Literature and Philosophy. University Park, Pa.: Pennsylvania State University Press, 1992.
Besançon, Alain. *The Forbidden Image: An Intellectual History of Iconoclasm.* Chicago: University of Chicago Press, 2000.
Blake, William. "'The Tyger' and 'The Lamb.'" Web Page for Romantic Circles High School Reader containing William Blake's "The Tyger" and "The Lamb" from *Songs of Innocence and of Experience, copy Z* [London: Printed by Catherine Blake and William Blake, 1789–1794, 1826].
Bréhier, Louis. *La Querelle Des Images (VIIIe-IXe Siècles).* New York: B. Franklin, 1969.
Brown, Peter. "Images as Substitute for Writing." In *East and West Modes of Communication: Proceedings of the First Plenary Conference at Merida,* vol. v. 5, edited by Euangelos K. Chrysos and I. N. Wood. Transformation of the Roman World. Leiden/Boston: Brill, 1999.
Bustard, Ned. *It Was Good Making Art to the Glory of God.* Baltimore, Md.: Square Halo Books, 2000.
Camfield, William. "Marcel Duchamp's Fountain: Aesthetic Object, Icon, or Anti-Art?" In *The Definitively Unfinished Marcel Duchamp,* edited by Thierry de Duve, 132–78. Halifax, N.S./Cambridge, Mass.: Nova Scotia College of Art and Design/MIT Press, 1991.
Campbell, Joseph. *Part 1: Primitive Hunters and Gatherers.* Vol. 1. The way of the animal powers of *Historical Atlas of World Mythology.* New York: Harper & Row, 1988.
Carruthers, Mary. *The Craft of Thought Meditation, Rhetoric, and the Making of Images, 400–1200.* Cambridge Studies in Medieval Literature. New York: Cambridge University Press, 1998.
Cassian, John, and Boniface Ramsey. *John Cassian, The Conferences.* Translated by Boniface Ramsey. Ancient Christian Writers. New York: Paulist Press, 1997.
Clark, Elizabeth A. *The Origenist Controversy: The Cultural Construction of an Early Christian Debate.* Princeton, N.J.: Princeton University Press, 1992.
Colonnese, Louis M., and the Catholic Church. *The Church in the Present-Day Transformation of Latin America in the Light of the Council Second General Conference of Latin American Bishops, Bogotá, 24 August, Medellin, 26 August–6 September, Colombia, 1968.* Bogota: General Secretariat of CELAM, 1970.
Crumley, Bruce. "Archaeology: Cave Art in France." *Time* 145, no. 5 (30 January 1995).

Culpepper, Robert H. *Interpreting the Atonement*. Grand Rapids, Mich.: Eerdmans, 1966.

Danto, Arthur Coleman. *The Transfiguration of the Commonplace a Philosophy of Art*. Cambridge, Mass.: Harvard University Press, 1981.

______. *After the End of Art: Contemporary Art and the Pale of History*. The A. W. Mellon Lectures in the Fine Arts. Princeton, N.J.: Princeton University Press, 1997.

______. *Beyond the Brillo Box: The Visual Arts in Post-Historical Perspective*. Berkeley: University of California Press, 1998.

Deck, Allan Fuigeroa, ed. *Frontiers of Hispanic Theology*. Maryknoll, N.Y.: Orbis Books, 1992.

de Medina, Bernardo, O.P. *San Martin de Porres: Biografía del Siglo XVII*. 1663. Mexico City: Editorial Jus, S.A., 1964.

de Pacchioni, Neri Romero. *La Fascinante Vida del Santo Martín de Porres*. Lima: Centro de Proyección Cristiana, n.d.

Dewey, John. *Art as Experience*. 1934. Perigee Books. New York: The Berkley Publishing Group, 1980.

Dillenberger, John. *A Theology of Artistic Sensibilities: The Visual Arts and the Church*. New York: Crossroad, 1986.

Donovan, Mary Ann. *One Right Reading? A Guide to Irenaeus*. Collegeville, Minn.: The Liturgical Press, 1997.

Dulles, Avery. "Two Languages of Salvation: The Lutheran–Catholic Joint Declaration." *First Things* 98 (December 1999) 25–30.

Dussel, Enrique, ed. *Introducción General a la Historia de la Iglesia en América Latina*. Vol. 1 of *Historia General de la Iglesia en América Latina*. CEHILA. Salamanca: Ediciones Sígueme, 1983.

Duve, Thierry de. *Nominalisme Pictural Marcel Duchamp, la Peinture et la Modernité*. Collection "Critique." Paris: Editions de Minuit, 1984.

Elizondo, Virgilio. "Our Lady of Guadalupe as a Cultural Symbol." In *Liturgy and Cultural Traditions*. Ed. Herman Power and David Schmidt, 25–33. N.Y.: Seabury Press, 1977.

______. *Guadalupe, Mother of the New Creation*. Maryknoll, N.Y.: Orbis Books, 1997.

Eodice, Alexander R. "Innocence Lost and Found." *American Catholic Philosophical Quarterly* 74, no. 2000 (2001) 299–305.

Espín, Orlando. "Religiosidad popular: unaporte para su definición y hermenéutica." *Estudios Sociales* 17 (October–December 1984) 41–54.

______. *The Faith of the People: Theological Reflections on Popular Catholicism*. Maryknoll, N.Y.: Orbis Books, 1997.

Fields, Stephens, S J. "Balthasar and Rahner on the Spiritual Senses." *Theological Studies* 57, no. 2 (June 1996) 224–41.

Finney, Paul Corby. *The Invisible God: The Earliest Christians on Art*. New York: Oxford University Press, 1994.

Freedberg, David. *The Power of Images Studies in the History and Theory of Response*. Chicago: University of Chicago Press, 1989.

Fuller, Peter, and Power Institute of Fine Arts. *Aesthetics After Modernism*. London, England/New York: Writers and Readers distributed in the U.S.A. by Norton, 1983.

Gablik, Suzi. *The Reenchantment of Art*. New York: Thames and Hudson, 1991.

García-Rivera, Alex. *St. Martín de Porres the "Little Stories" and the Semiotics of Culture*. Faith and Cultures Series. Maryknoll, N.Y.: Orbis Books, 1995.

______. *The Community of the Beautiful: A Theological Aesthetics*. Collegeville, Minn.: The Liturgical Press, 1999.

______. Personal conversation. Interview with Arthur Poulin, O.S.B. Cam. Incarnation Monastery, 2001.

Gelpi, Donald L. *Doctrinal and Practical Christology*. Vol. 3 of *The Firstborn of Many: A Christology for Converting Christians*. Marquette Studies in Theology. Milwaukee: Marquette University Press, 2001.

______. *The Gracing of Human Experience: Rethinking the Relationship Between Nature and Grace*. Collegeville, Minn.: The Liturgical Press, 2001.

Gerbi, Antonello. *The Dispute of the New World: The History of a Polemic, 1750–1900*. Translation of: *La disputa del Nuovo Mono: Storia di una polemica, 1750–1900,* original work published in Italy, 1955. Translated and revised by Jeremy Moyle. Pittsburg: University of Pittsburgh Press, 1973.

Giakalis, Ambrosios. *Images of the Divine: The Theology of Icons at the Seventh Ecumenical Council*. Studies in the History of Christian Thought. Leiden/New York: E. J. Brill, 1994.

Girard, René. *La Violence et le Sacré.* Paris: B. Grasset, 1972.

______. *The Scapegoat*. Baltimore: Johns Hopkins University Press, 1986.

Girard, René, Jean-Michel Oughourlian, and Guy Lefort. *Things Hidden Since the Foundation of the World*. Stanford, Calif.: Stanford University Press, 1987.

Goizueta, Roberto S. *We Are a People: Initiatives in Hispanic American Theology*. Edited by Roberto S. Goizueta. Minneapolis: Fortress Press, 1992.

______. *Caminemos con Jesús: Toward a Hispanic/Latino Theology of Accompaniment*. Maryknoll, N.Y.: Orbis Books, 1995.

Gombrich, E. H. *Art and Illusion: A Study in the Psychology of Pictorial Representation*. A. W. Mellon lectures in the fine arts, 1956. Bollingen Series. New York: Pantheon Books, 1961.

Gorringe, Timothy. *God's Just Vengeance: Crime, Violence, and the Rhetoric of Salvation*. Cambridge Studies in Ideology and Religion. Cambridge/New York: Cambridge University Press, 1996.

Grabar, André. *Christian Iconography: A Study of Its Origins.* Princeton, N.J.: Princeton University Press, 1968.

______. *L'Iconoclasme Byzantin: Le Dossier Archéologique*. Paris: Flammarion, 1984.

Gutiérrez, Gustavo. "Prologue." In *Religión del Pobre y Liberación en Chimbote,* edited by Diego Irarrazaval. Lima: Centrod de Estudios y Publicaciones, 1978.

Hale, Robert, O.S.B. Cam. "Camaldolese Spirituality." In *The New Dictionary of Catholic Spirituality,* edited by Michael Downey, 107–10. Collegeville, Minn.: The Liturgical Press, 1993.

______. "Eremitical Life." In *The New Dictionary of Catholic Spirituality,* edited by Michael Downey, 352–54. Collegeville, Minn.: The Liturgical Press, 1993.

Hanke, Lewis. *Aristotle and the American Indians: A Study in Race Prejudice in the Modern World.* Bloomington, Ind.: Indiana University Press, 1959.

Harrison, Carol. *Beauty and Revelation in the Thought of Saint Augustine.* Oxford Theological Monographs. Oxford [England]/New York: Clarendon Press/Oxford University Press, 1992.

Hass, Kristin Ann. *Carried to the Wall American Memory and the Vietnam Veterans Memorial.* Berkeley: University of California Press, 1998.

Hegel, Georg Wilhelm Friedrich, Bernard Bosanquet, and M. J. Inwood. *Introductory Lectures on Aesthetics.* Edited by M. J. Inwood. Translated by Bernard Bosanquet. Penguin Classics. London/New York: Penguin Books, 1993.

Hibbard, Howard. *Caravaggio.* New York: Harper & Row, 1983.

Hinks, R. P. *Michelangelo Merisi da Caravaggio: His Life, His Legend, His Works.* New York: Beechhurst Press, 1953.

Irarrazaval, Diego. "Cristianos en el Proceso Socialista." In *Cristianos por Socialismo,* edited by Reues Mate Ruperez, 413–86. Estella: Editorial Verbo Divino, 1975.

James, William. *The Varieties of Religious Experience: A Study in Human Nature.* New York: Longmans, Green, 1902.

Jensen, Robin Margaret. *Understanding Early Christian Art.* London/New York: Routledge, 2000.

John Paul II. "Letter to Artists." *Origins* 28, no. 46 (1999) 786–93.

Kelsey, David H. "Human Being." In *Christian Theology: An Introduction,* edited by Alister E. McGrath. Oxford, UK/Cambridge, Mass.: Blackwell, 1994.

Kessler, Herbert L. *Spiritual Seeing: Picturing God's Invisibility in Medieval Art.* The Middle Ages Series. Philadelphia: University of Pennsylvania Press, 2000.

Kittel, Gerhard Friedrich, ed. "Kalypto." In *Theological Dictionary of the New Testament Abridged in One Volume.* 1985. Michigan: Logos Research Systems, Inc., 1995–99.

Lambrecht, J., S.J. "Beatitudes." In *The New Dictionary of Catholic Spirituality,* edited by Michael Downey, 78–83. Collegeville, Minn.: The Liturgical Press, 1993.

Lindberg, David C. *Theories of Vision from al-Kindi to Kepler.* Chicago: University of Chicago Press, 1976.

Lindskoog, Kathryn Ann, and Dante Alighieri. *Purgatory: Journey to Joy, Part Two*. Vol. 2 of *Dante's Divine Comedy*. Retold, with notes by Kathryn Lindskoog. Macon, Ga.: Mercer University Press, 1997.

Lotz, Johannes Baptist. "Transcendentals." In *Sacramentum Mundi,* vol. 6, edited by Karl Rahner, 285–87. New York: Herder and Herder, 1970.

Louth, Andrew. *Denys, the Areopagite*. Wilton, Conn.: Morehouse, 1989.

Lowe, Walter James. "Innocence and Experience." In *Evil Self and Culture,* vol. 4, edited by Marie Coleman. Nelson and Michael Eigen. Self-In-Process, 239–67. New York: Human Sciences Press, 1984.

Maritain, Jacques. *Art and Scholasticism, and The Frontiers of Poetry*. New York: Scribner, 1962.

______. *Creative Intuition in Art and Poetry*. A. W. Mellon Lectures in the Fine Arts. Princeton Guildford: Princeton University Press, 1977.

Mathews, Thomas F. *The Clash of Gods: A Reinterpretation of Early Christian Art*. Princeton, N.J.: Princeton University Press, 1999.

Matus, Thomas, Peter Damian, and Bruno. *The Mystery of Romuald and the Five Brothers: Stories from the Benedictines and Camaldolese*. Trabuco Canyon, Calif.: Source Books, 1994.

McDonald, H. D. *The Atonement of the Death of Christ in Faith, Revelation, and History*. Grand Rapids, Mich.: Baker Book House, 1985.

McGrath, Alister E. *Iustitia Dei: A History of the Christian Doctrine of Justification*. Cambridge, U.K./New York: Cambridge University Press, 1998.

Merton, Thomas. *Contemplative Prayer*. Garden City, N.Y.: Image Books, 1971.

Miles, Margaret. "Vision: The Eye of Body and the Eye of the Mind in St. Augustine's *De Trinitate* and the *Confessions." Journal of Religion* 163, no. 2 (April 1983) 125–42.

Miles, Margaret Ruth. *Image as Insight: Visual Understanding in Western Christianity and Secular Culture*. Boston: Beacon Press, 1985.

Miller, Perry. *Jonathan Edwards*. Amherst, Mich.: University of Massachusetts Press, 1981.

Morgan, David. *Visual Piety: A History and Theory of Popular Religious Images*. Berkeley: University of California Press, 1998.

Newman, John Henry Cardinal. *An Essay in Aid of a Grammar of Assent*. With an introduction by Nicholas Lash. Notre Dame, Ind.: University of Notre Dame Press, 1979.

Oberman, Heiko Augustinus. *The Harvest of Medieval Theology: Gabriel Biel and Late Medieval Nominalism*. Rev. ed. Grand Rapids, Mich.: William B. Eerdmans, 1967.

O'Rourke, Fran. *Pseudo-Dionysius and the Metaphysics of Aquinas*. Studien und Texte Zur Geistesgeschichte Des Mittelalters. Leiden/New York: E. J. Brill, 1992.

Pagden, Anthony. *The Fall of Natural Man: The American Indian and the Origin of Comparative Ethnology*. 1982. Cambridge Iberian and Latin American Studies. Cambridge: Cambridge University Press, 1986.

Panofsky, Erwin. *Gothic Architecture and Scholasticism*. New York: Meridian Books, 1957.

Pattison, George. *Art, Modernity, and Faith: Restoring the Image*. London: SCM Press, 1998.

Pelikan, Jaroslav Jan. *Imago Dei: The Byzantine Apologia for Icons*. Washington, D.C., National Gallery of Art. Princeton, N.J.: Princeton University Press, 1990.

Pfeiffer, John E. *The Creative Explosion: An Inquiry Into the Origins of Art and Religion*. New York: Harper & Row, 1982.

Pseudo-Dionysius, Colm Luibhéid, and Paul. Rorem. *Pseudo-Dionysius: The Complete Works*. Translated by Colm Luibhéid. New York: Paulist Press, 1987.

Rahner, Karl. "La Doctrine des 'Sens Spirituels' au Moyen-Age." *Revue d'Ascétique et de Mystique* 14, no. 55 (1933) 263–99.

______. "Theology and the Arts." *Thought* 57 (1982).

Ricard, Robert. *The Spiritual Conquest of Mexico*. Originally published in French as *Conquête Spirituelle de Mexique,* published as volume XX of *Travaux et Mémoires de L'institute d'Ethnologie* by the University of Paris. Translated by Lesley Bird Simpson. California Library reprint. Berkeley: University of California Press, 1966.

Richard, Pablo, Enrique D. Dussel, Comisión de Estudios de Historia de la Iglesia en Latinoamérica, and Departamento Ecuménico de Investigaciones (Costa Rica). *Materiales para una Historia de la Teología en América Latina*. Edited by Pablo Richard. San José, Costa Rica: Comisión de Estudios de Historia de la Iglesia en América Latina Departamento Ecuménico de Investigaciones, 1981.

Richard, Pablo, Carmelo Alvarez, and Comisión de Estudios de Historia de la Iglesia en Latinoamérica. *Raíces de la Teología Latinoamericana Nuevos Materiales para la Historia de la Teología*. Edited by Pablo Richard. San José, Costa Rica: CEHILA Departamento Ecuménico de Investigaciones, 1985.

Robb, Peter. *M the Man Who Became Caravaggio*. New York: Henry Holt, 2000.

Roman Catholic Church and Lutheran World Federation. "Joint Declaration on the Doctrine of Justification." Online reference of full text of the Declaration and related Official Common Statement.

Rondet, Henri. *Original Sin: The Patristic and Theological Background*. Shannon: Ecclesia Press, 1972.

Roques, René. *L'Univers Dionysien Structure Hiérarchique Du Monde Selon le Pseudo-Denys*. Théologie. Paris: Aubier, 1954.

Rorem, Paul. *Pseudo-Dionysius a Commentary on the Texts and an Introduction to Their Influence*. New York: Oxford University Press, 1993.

Royce, Josiah. *The Sources of Religious Insight Lectures*. New York: Scribner, 1912.

Royce, Josiah, and John Clendenning. *The Letters of Josiah Royce.* Edited by John Clendenning. Chicago: University of Chicago Press, 1970.

Rudolph, Conrad, and Bernard. *The "Things of Greater Importance": Bernard of Clairvaux's Apologia and the Medieval Attitude Toward Art*. Philadelphia: University of Pennsylvania Press, 1990.

Sabourin, Leopold. *Rédemption Sacrificielle une Enquête Exégétique*. Bruges: Desclée de Brouwer, 1961.

San Martin de Porres. Vol. 1 of *Bilioteca Hombres del Peru*. Edited by Hernan Alva Orlandini. Lima: La Oficina Tecnica Editorial de Edif. Caucato, 1964.

Scarry, Elaine. *On Beauty and Being Just*. Princeton, N.J.: Princeton University Press, 1999.

Schaeffer, Jean-Marie. *Art of the Modern Age: Philosophy of Art from Kant to Heidegger*. New French Thought. Princeton, N.J.: Princeton University Press, 2000.

Schönborn, Christoph von. *God's Human Face the Christ-Icon*. San Francisco: Ignatius Press, 1994.

Scruggs, Jan C., and Joel L. Swerdlow. *To Heal a Nation: The Vietnam Veterans Memorial*. New York: Harper & Row, 1985.

Secretariado Martín de Porres. Translation from the Latin into Spanish of the official Process of Beatification of St. Martin of Porres during the years 1660–1674 in *Proceso de Beatificación de Fray Martín de Porres*. 1660–71. Palencia: Secretatiado "Martin de Porres," 1960.

Simson, Otto Georg von. *The Gothic Cathedral: Origins of Gothic Architecture and the Medieval Concept of Order*. Bollingen Series. New York: Pantheon Books, 1962.

Spencer, Duncan, and Lloyd Wolf. *Facing the Wall: Americans at the Vietnam Veterans Memorial.* New York/London: Macmillan/Collier Macmillan, 1986.

Suger, and Erwin Panofsky. *Abbot Suger on the Abbey Church of St.-Denis and Its Art Treasures.* Edited by Erwin Panofsky. Princeton, N.J.: Princeton University Press, 1948.

Tambasco, Anthony J. *A Theology of Atonement and Paul's Vision of Christianity*. Collegeville, Minn.: The Liturgical Press, 1991.

Tillich, Paul. *Existence and the Christ*. Vol. 2 of *Systematic Theology.* Chicago: University of Chicago Press, 1957.

______. *Theology of Culture*. Edited by Robert C. Kimball. New York: Oxford University Press, Galaxy, 1964.

______. *The Courage to Be*. Yale Nota Bene. New Haven, Conn.: Yale University Press, 2000.

Tillich, Paul, Jane Dillenberger, and John Dillenberger. *On Art and Architecture*. Edited by Jane Dillenberger. Translated by Jane Dillenberger. New York: Crossroad, 1987.

Tomkins, Calvin, and Time-Life Books. *The World of Marcel Duchamp, 1887–1968*. Edited by Time-Life Books. Alexandria, Va./Morristown, N.J.: Time-Life Books school and library distribution by Silver Burdett Co., 1977.

United States Catholic Conference. *The Catechism of the Catholic Church*. Vatican City: Libreria Editrice Vaticana, 1994.

Vigilucci, Lino. *Camaldoli: A Journey Into Its History & Spirituality*. Trabuco Canyon, Calif.: Source Books Hermitage Books, 1995.

Wittgenstein, Ludwig, G. H. von Wright, and Heikki Nyman. *Culture and Value*. Edited by G. H. von Wright. Chicago: University of Chicago Press, 1980.

Wolgast, Elizabet. "Innocence." *Philosophy* 68 (1993) 297–307.

Wolter, Allan Bernard. *The Transcendentals and Their Function in the Metaphysics of Duns Scotus*. Washington, D.C.: The Catholic University of America Press, 1946.

Zajonc, Arthur. *Catching the Light: The Entwined History of Light and Mind*. New York: Bantam Books, 1993.

Index

8794